THE SUCCESS BOOK

Ebere Nicodemus Oduaro

TABLE OF CONTENTS

Chapter 1 ………………….. 5

What are Success Codes?

Chapter 2 ………………….. 39

Unlocking Your Potential

Chapter 3 ………………….. 65

Mastering the Art of Productivity

Chapter 4 ………………….. 99

Cultivating Resilience

Chapter 5 ………………….. 123

Building Strong Relationships

Chapter 6 ………………….. 151

Creating a Positive Mindset

Chapter 7 ………………….. 176

Embracing Continuous Learning

Chapter 8 ………………….. 198

Enjoying a Life of Success

Key Concepts Covered in the Book

Additional Resources for Readers

Chapter 1

What are Success Codes?

Success means different things to different people. It is a subjective concept seen or explained in some ways by different people based on their values, goals, and aspirations. To some, success means having a lot of money in their bank accounts. For some, it means having a great marriage and great children. To some, success is having a great career and doing well in it, while to others, success means having a great business and thriving in it. Thus, it is necessary to find out what success means to you. What would you have achieved to feel that you are successful?

One thing I want you to remember is that to be successful, you need to set goals. People who are successful in life are usually goal-oriented. They set goals and work towards achieving those goals. They know what they want and focus on working hard and working smart to achieve it. Your ability to set goals is the master skill of success. When you set goals for different areas of your life and work towards achieving them, you have set yourself up for success. The moment you start to achieve these goals, that feeling of fulfilment rubs off on you and other areas of your life. It can make you feel successful.

The truth is, it does not matter your background and the things you have been through or even your present situation or circumstance; what matters most is that you have a destination in mind, know how to get there, and are focused on getting there. That is why it is good to set goals. Goals are the roadmap to your success. Whenever you set goals, it increases your confidence and boosts your ability to be motivated to achieve those goals.

At its core, success is the achievement of desired outcomes, the fulfilment of one's goals, and the realization of personal satisfaction and happiness.

Success cuts across various aspects of life, including personal, professional, financial and social dimensions. Success is not only determined by external parameters such as wealth, fame, or status but also by internal parameters. The internal parameters include personal growth, well-being, and ability to impact oneself and others positively. These external and internal parameters make up the codes you need to achieve these successes.

Success codes, therefore, refer to a set of principles, strategies, and habits that successful individuals use to achieve their goals and attain full life potential. These codes include a range of practices such as goal-setting, time management, developing a positive mindset, building relationships, cultivating resilience, continuous learning, and more. Success codes are based on the experiences and insights of successful people who have achieved significant accomplishments in their personal or professional lives. By learning and applying these success codes, individuals can develop the skills and mindset needed to achieve their goals and create a life of success. The first step is to have a success mindset.

A Success Mindset

Your mind is where it all starts from. Everything you see around you is the product of a thought. Somebody somewhere thought of a pain, a concern or a phenomenon and turned that thought into a solution. Everything in life started as a dream, a hope or a wish that turned into reality.

Thoughts are things, and thoughts are creative. Your thoughts form and shape your world and everything that happens to you. That is why the Bible says you should guard your heart jealously because out of the heart flows the issues of life. Your mind is so powerful that you become what you think about most of the time. What dominates your thoughts most of the time eventually becomes your reality. Thus, it is good to develop a positive mindset about success. When you have a positive mindset about success, it will become a reality. But, if you always see yourself struggling, and you accept and confess it, that is what will happen to you.

Do you know why wealthy people get wealthier while poor people get poorer? Successful people always think about what solutions they can provide to get paid for it. Thus, they are constantly expanding their businesses, diversifying, building more businesses and multiple inflows of earnings. The less visionary in society think only of what they can eat daily and do not think of starting and building a business.

It is important to note that people who talk about their problems and sorrows always remain in it. Successful people who make positive confessions and keep their thoughts and conversations on a high level excel. They usually succeed and experience the good things they think about and confess.

Control Your Thoughts and Words

To ensure your mindset positions you for success, you are to control your thoughts and words. You must keep your mind positive. You must refuse to talk badly about other people or situations. If you cannot approach the person and talk about it or help overcome the bad attitude or action they put up, then keep your mouth shut. Refuse to join other people to criticize such a person, complain about them or condemn them. Why is this so important? Whenever you criticize, complain, or condemn someone, you cause yourself more harm. The act of complaint and criticism will trigger negative emotions inside you, which range from irritation to frustration to anger to hatred for that person. But the thing is that you will be the sufferer of these negative emotions, not the person you are thinking them towards. Your negativity does not affect the other person but you at all times. The reason you should control your thoughts and actions and make sure they are positive all the time. Being angry with someone is tantamount to allowing the person to control your emotions, thoughts, and words. You should know that positive emotions empower and make you feel powerful and successful, while negative emotions make you irritable.

Identifying Your Unique Strengths and Talents

Identifying your unique strengths and talents is a yardstick to achieving success. Below are some strategies to help you discover your strengths and talents:

1. **Take assessments:** Various assessments can help you identify your strengths and talents. Some of the assessments include Strengths Finder, Myers-Briggs Type Indicator, and Clifton Strengths. They can help you gain insight into your personality, natural talents, and areas of strength.
2. **Reflect on your past experiences:** Think about your past experiences and identify the tasks you enjoyed doing and excelled at. What activities did you receive positive

feedback for? These can give you clues to your natural strengths and talents.

3. **Ask others for feedback:** Sometimes, others see our strengths and talents better than we do. Ask people who know you well to give you honest feedback on what they believe your strengths and talent are.

4. **Pay attention to what energizes you:** When you engage in certain activities, kindly pay attention to how you feel. Do you feel energized and motivated? What tasks give you a sense of purpose and fulfilment? These can be indicators of your strengths and talents.

5. **Experiment with different activities:** We may not know our strengths and talents until we attempt different tasks. Attempt

different tasks or activities and see how you enjoyed and excelled in the tasks undertaken. This attitude can help you discover new strengths and talents you may not have been aware of before.

Remember, discovering your strengths and talents is an ongoing process. Keep exploring and trying new things, and you will continue to uncover new aspects of yourself.

Significance of Achieving Success

Success is a multifaceted term that holds different meanings for different people. To one, success could mean achieving personal goals and professional milestones and fulfilling dreams to another. The significance of attaining success goes beyond external validation. In this submission, we will delve into the profound relevance of achieving success and how it impacts various aspects of our lives. From personal growth and self-esteem to having a positive impact and leaving a lasting legacy, success plays a transformative role in unlocking our full potential and shaping a fulfilling and purposeful existence.

1. **Personal Growth and Fulfillment:** Achieving success serves as a motivation for personal growth and fulfilment. As we strive towards our goals and overcome challenges, we learn valuable lessons, develop new skills, and expand our capabilities. Each accomplishment reinforces our belief in our abilities and fuels our desire for continuous growth. Success brings a sense of fulfilment and satisfaction.

2. **Increased Confidence and Self-Esteem:** Success breeds confidence and boosts self-esteem. As we achieve our goals, we gain a sense of self-assurance. Accomplishing what we set out to do reinforces our belief that we can overcome challenges and obstacles. This confidence spills over into other areas of our lives, enabling us to take on new ventures, face adversity with resilience, and pursue even greater aspirations.

3. **Motivation and Drive:** Success fuels motivation and drive. When we taste the sweet fruits of success, we are inspired to push our limits further and aim higher. Each achievement serves as a reminder of what we can accomplish when we apply ourselves and remain dedicated. Success

becomes a driving force, propelling us forward and igniting a fire within us to pursue excellence.

4. **Influencing and Inspiring Others:** Achieving success can influence and inspire others. When we demonstrate that success is attainable through hard work, perseverance, and resilience, we serve as role models for those around us. Our achievements can inspire others to believe in their potential, and motivate them to set goals and pursue those goals. By sharing our experiences and knowledge, we can positively impact the lives of others and contribute to a culture of success and personal empowerment.

5. **Creating Opportunities and Financial Stability:** Success opens doors to new opportunities and financial stability. Accomplishing goals often leads to recognition, advancement, and access to new ventures. Success brings an expanded network, connecting us with like-minded individuals, mentors, and potential collaborators. Financial stability is another significant aspect of success, providing us with the means to enjoy a comfortable life, support our loved ones, and pursue further aspirations.
6. **Leaving a Lasting Legacy:** Success allows us to leave a lasting legacy. When we achieve significant milestones or have an impact on others and society, we create a lasting imprint that extends beyond our

lifetime. Whether this impact is through groundbreaking inventions, artistic creations, philanthropic endeavours, or inspiring leadership, success enables us to make a meaningful contribution to the world, leaving a legacy that will be remembered and appreciated by future generations.

7. **Personal Satisfaction and Happiness:** Ultimately, achieving success brings personal satisfaction and happiness. It is the realization of our dreams, the culmination of our efforts, and the affirmation that we live a life aligned with our passions and values. Success allows us to live authentically, pursue our interests, and create a sense of balance and fulfilment. It brings joy and contentment

that transcends material possessions or external accolades.

The significance of achieving success goes beyond personal accolades or societal recognition. It is a transformative journey that enhances personal growth, builds confidence, and fuels motivation. Success can inspire others, create opportunities, and leave a lasting legacy. Success brings personal satisfaction, happiness, and a deep sense of fulfilment. Embrace the journey, unlock your full potential, and enjoy the profound significance of achieving success in all its forms.

Importance of a Success Mindset

A success mindset is a powerful tool that can propel individuals towards achieving their goals and creating a life of fulfilment and accomplishment. It involves cultivating a positive and empowering mental framework that supports growth, resilience, and a belief in one's ability to overcome challenges. We will navigate the importance of having a success mindset and probe into the concept of success codes—strategies and principles that can help develop and strengthen this mindset. By embracing a success mindset and implementing success codes, individuals can unlock their full potential and navigate their journey towards success with confidence and determination.

1. **Shaping Perception and Beliefs:** A success mindset begins with shaping perception and beliefs. It involves adopting a positive outlook and reframing challenges as learning points

and an avenue for growth. By replacing limiting beliefs with empowering ones, individuals can develop a mindset that believes in their potential for success. Success codes, such as affirmations, visualization, and positive self-talk, play a crucial role in reshaping perception and reinforcing positive beliefs.

2. **Cultivating Resilience and Persistence:** A success mindset is characterized by resilience and persistence in the face of setbacks and obstacles. It involves embracing failure as a tool for success and persevering through difficult times. Success codes like embracing failure as a learning opportunity, developing a growth mindset, and setting realistic expectations help individuals bounce

back from setbacks and stay focused on their goals.

3. **Embracing a Growth Mindset:** A growth mindset is a subset of the success mindset. This mindset allows individuals to view challenges as learning points to develop and improve new skills and competencies. Success codes such as embracing lifelong learning, seeking feedback, and embracing discomfort facilitate the development of a growth mindset and pave the way for continuous personal and professional growth.

4. **Setting Clear Goals and Taking Action:** Haven a success mindset involves setting clear goals and taking consistent action towards their attainment. Success codes like setting SMART goals, breaking them

down into actionable steps, and developing a strategic plan help individuals clarify their objectives and take purposeful action. By aligning actions with goals, individuals progress and build momentum towards success.

5. **Building a Supportive Network:** A success mindset is nurtured through a supportive network of like-minded individuals. Surrounding oneself with positive and supportive people who encourage growth, provide inspiration, and share similar values can significantly impact one's mindset. Success codes such as networking, seeking mentorship, and participating in mastermind groups facilitate the creation of a supportive

network that fosters personal and professional growth.

6. **Overcoming Fear and Embracing Risk:** A success mindset involves overcoming fear and embracing risk-taking. Success codes such as reframing fear as excitement, embracing calculated risks, and stepping outside their comfort zones enable individuals to break free from limiting beliefs and take bold actions. By pushing through discomfort, individuals can expand their horizons and seize opportunities for success.

7. **Celebrating Milestones and Practicing Gratitude:** A success mindset involves celebrating milestones, no matter how small, and practising gratitude for the journey. Success codes such as

acknowledging achievements, expressing gratitude for progress, and celebrating efforts and dedication help individuals maintain a positive mindset and cultivate a sense of accomplishment.

A success mindset is a transformative mindset that empowers individuals to navigate their path towards success. Embracing success codes and implementing strategies that shape perception, cultivate resilience, foster growth, set clear goals, build support networks, overcome fear, and celebrate milestones help individuals develop and strengthen their success mindset. With a success mindset, individuals can unlock their full potential, navigate challenges easily, and create a life of purpose, fulfilment, and accomplishment.

12 Proven Strategies to Achieve Success in Life

Success is a subjective concept. Whether success means achieving personal goals, professional accomplishments, or a sense of fulfilment, some tips can support individuals on their journey to success. In this comprehensive guide, we will explore twelve effective ways to succeed. By implementing these strategies, individuals can develop the mindset, habits, and actions necessary to achieve their desired success and create a life of purpose, meaning, and accomplishment.

1. **Define Your Vision and Set Clear Goals:** To succeed, you should make your vision and goals plain. Take time to reflect on your values, passions, and aspirations.

Visualize what success looks like for you in different areas of life. Set Specific, Measurable, Achievable, Relevant, and Time-limit (SMART) goals that align with your vision. Clear goals provide direction, focus, and motivation to succeed.

2. **Develop a Growth Mindset:** A growth mindset can bring success. View challenges as learning points for growth. Emphasize the process rather than the outcome. Cultivate resilience, perseverance, and a willingness to take risks. This mindset strengthens you to overcome obstacles, learn from failures, and improve.

3. **Take Action and Embrace Failure:** Success requires consistent action and the willingness to embrace failure.

Procrastination and fear of failure can hinder progress. Take the initiative and step out of your comfort zone. Learn from failures and use them as tools for success. Embrace a mindset of experimentation and iterate based on feedback and results. Taking action, even in the face of uncertainty, creates momentum and opens doors to opportunities.

4. **Cultivate Self-Discipline and Consistency:** Self-discipline and consistency are factors for success. Develop habits that support your goals and eliminate distractions that hinder progress. Create a schedule or routine that enables you to prioritize and focus on tasks. Stay committed to your goals even when motivation wanes. Practice delayed

gratification by sacrificing short-term pleasures for long-term success. Consistent efforts and disciplined actions build momentum and pave the way for achievement.

5. **Seek Continuous Learning and Personal Growth:** Success requires a commitment to continuous learning and personal growth. Stay curious and seek opportunities for self-improvement. Be a reader, attend meetings such as talks, workshops, symposia, and seminars, enrol in courses, and participate in activities that expand your knowledge, competencies and skills. Seek feedback and give room for constructive criticism. Embrace a mindset of lifelong learning

and adopt a growth-oriented approach to personal development.

6. **Build a Strong Support Network:** Have a strong support network and system that challenges and inspires you. Connect with like-minded with shared goals and values. Seek mentors who can provide guidance and wisdom based on their experiences. Collaborate with individuals who complement your strengths and help you overcome weaknesses. A supportive network provides encouragement, accountability, and valuable insights that can propel you towards success.

7. **Develop Effective Communication Skills:** Effective communication skills are crucial for success in various facets of life. Develop the ability to articulate your

thoughts, listen actively, and express yourself clearly and confidently. Enhance your interpersonal skills to build strong relationships and collaborate effectively. Communicate your ideas, goals, and needs with clarity and empathy. Effective communication fosters understanding, resolves conflicts, and creates opportunities for growth and success.

8. **Cultivate Emotional Intelligence:** Emotional intelligence plays a significant role in achieving success. Develop self-awareness to understand your emotions, strengths, and weaknesses. Practice self-regulation to manage your emotions effectively and respond constructively to challenges. Cultivate empathy to understand and connect with others on a

deeper level. Develop strong interpersonal skills to build meaningful relationships and navigate social dynamics successfully.

9. **Embrace a Positive Mindset:** A positive mindset is essential for success. Cultivate optimism, gratitude, and a belief in your ability to overcome obstacles. Focus on finding solutions and do not dwell on problems. Practice positive self-talk and affirmations to reinforce empowering beliefs. Surround yourself with positivity through inspirational materials, uplifting relationships, and gratitude practices. A positive mindset enhances resilience, motivation, and overall well-being.

10. **Practice Time Management and Prioritization:** Time management and

prioritization are skills needed for success. Kindly learn to manage your time effectively by prioritizing tasks, setting deadlines, and eliminating time-wasting activities. Attend to tasks early and do not allow them to become urgent. Identify your most important goals and allocate time and energy accordingly. Use productivity techniques like the Pomodoro Technique or time-blocking to maximize focus and efficiency. Develop the ability to balance competing demands and make conscious choices on how you use your time.

11. **Embrace Adaptability and Change:** Success often requires adaptability and the ability to change. Being open to new ideas, perspectives, and opportunities is

crucial. Be willing to step outside your comfort zone, learn new skills, and adapt to changing circumstances. Embrace a growth mindset that sees change as a chance for growth and improvement. Develop resilience and flexibility to navigate uncertainty and turn challenges into opportunities.

12. **Take Care of Your Well-being:** Achieving success goes beyond external accomplishments; it encompasses holistic well-being. Prioritize self-care by paying attention to your physical, mental, and emotional health and well-being. Maintain a balanced lifestyle, regular exercise, eat healthy, have a restful sleep, and manage your stress level. Practice mindfulness and relaxation techniques to

cultivate mental and emotional well-being. Take breaks and pursue hobbies that bring joy and rejuvenation. Taking care of your well-being ensures you have the energy, focus, and resilience necessary to pursue success sustainably.

Achieving success is a personal journey, but some tips can support individuals to reach their goals and create a fulfilling and accomplished life. By defining your vision, developing a growth mindset, taking action, cultivating discipline, yearning for continuous learning, building a support network, honing communication skills, nurturing emotional intelligence, embracing a positive mindset, mastering time management, adapting to change, and prioritizing well-being, you can lay a strong foundation for success in several areas of your life. Embrace these strategies and unlock your potential for success. Success is a lifelong journey where dedication and perseverance will enable you to achieve your desired life.

Chapter 2

Unlocking Your Potential

Within each individual lies untapped potential waiting to be unlocked. The journey of unlocking potential involves discovering and developing one's innate abilities, talents, and strengths to reach new heights of personal and professional growth. This article explores the process of unlocking potential and provides practical strategies to help individuals unleash their true capabilities. By embarking on this transformative journey, individuals can tap into their hidden reservoirs of talent to achieve great success and lead a more fulfilling life.

The first step in unlocking potential is self-discovery and reflection. Take time to delve deep within yourself to understand your values, passions, interests, and aspirations. Reflect on past experiences and moments of joy and fulfilment. Identify recurring patterns and themes that indicate areas where you excel. Self-awareness is the foundation upon which you can build your journey towards unlocking your true potential.

Adopting a growth mindset is essential for unlocking potential. Understand that competencies and skills can be developed and expanded through effort, perseverance, and a commitment to learning. See life issues as learning points for growth and view setbacks as stepping stones to success. Cultivate resilience, optimism, and a hunger for continuous improvement. A growth mindset empowers you to break free from self-imposed limitations and embrace your full potential. Setting inspiring goals is crucial in unlocking potential. Define clear and meaningful objectives that align with your values and aspirations. Set short-term and long-term goals that challenge you to stretch beyond your comfort zone. Goals provide direction and focus, motivating you to tap into your untapped potential.

Identifying and Leveraging Your Unique Strengths and Talents

Every individual possesses a unique set of strengths and talents that, when identified and harnessed, can be instrumental in achieving success and fulfilment. This section addresses practical tips or strategies for identifying and leveraging your unique strengths and talents. By embracing and capitalizing on what sets you apart, you can unmask your full potential, enhance your performance, and create a life that aligns with your passions and values.

- **Self-Reflection and Assessment:** These are crucial starting points for identifying your strengths and talents. Kindly introspect and evaluate your experiences, accomplishments, and areas where you excel. Consider activities that interest you and bring you a sense of fulfilment. Reflect on feedback from others regarding your strengths and areas of expertise. Self-assessment tools and personality assessments can also provide valuable insights into your natural inclinations and strengths.

- **Seek Feedback from Others:** Engage in open and honest conversations with trusted friends, colleagues, and mentors to gain a broader perspective on your strengths and talents. Observations and feedback can shed light on qualities and abilities you may have overlooked or undervalued. Pay attention to recurring compliments and recognition, as they often highlight areas of strength and talent.

- **Embrace a Growth Mindset:** This is crucial for leveraging your strengths and talents. You can enhance your skills through deliberate effort, learning, and practice. Even though you have natural strengths, there is always room for growth and improvement. Cultivate a mindset that embraces challenges, persists through setbacks, and seeks continuous development.
- **Identify Your Passion and Talents:** Passion and talent are indicators or directions to your purpose. Reflect on what genuinely excites and motivates you. Consider the activities or subjects that make you lose track of time and feel

deeply engaged. Aligning your strengths with your purpose can fuel your drive and provide a sense of fulfilment.

- **Experiment and Explore:** Do not be afraid to explore new activities, hobbies, and experiences to uncover hidden strengths and talents. Occasionally, vacate your comfort zone and take on new challenges. Engaging in diverse experiences can reveal previously untapped abilities and broaden your skill set. Embrace a mindset of curiosity and openness to continuous learning and growth.
- **Seek Opportunities for Skill Development:** Once you have identified your strengths and talents, seek opportunities to enhance and develop them. Invest in skill-building activities,

workshops, courses, or mentorship programs that align with your areas of strength. Acquiring knowledge and honing your skills will enhance your confidence and effectiveness.

- **Build a Supportive Network:** Locate and build a network that appreciates your strengths and talents. Connect with persons who can inspire and challenge you to grow. Identify and interact with mentors who can provide guidance and help you refine your abilities. Collaboration with like-minded individuals can provide opportunities for synergy and collective growth.
- **Leverage Strengths in Personal and Professional Life:** Identify ways to leverage your strengths and talents; this

can either be personal or in your professional life. For your career, seek roles and projects that align with your expertise. Look for opportunities to contribute your unique abilities to team efforts. In personal relationships, kindly know that your strengths can positively impact your interactions and the lives of others. Find ways to use your talents in hobbies and creative pursuits.

- **Develop a Growth Plan:** Create a plan that captures specific actions and milestones. Set clear objectives and establish a timeline for achieving them. Break down your plan into smaller, manageable steps to maintain momentum and track progress. Evaluate your growth plan and adjust to improve on it if necessary.

- **Embrace Lifelong Learning:** Continuously invest in your personal and professional development to unlock the full potential of your strengths and talents. Stay updated on industry trends, acquire new knowledge, and develop complementary skills. Seek feedback and opportunities for growth and improvement. Embracing lifelong learning ensures you can adapt to changing circumstances and be open to emerging opportunities.

Identifying and leveraging your unique strengths and talents is a transformative process that can lead to personal and professional success. Through self-reflection, feedback, a growth mindset and commitment to continuous learning; you can uncover your innate abilities and align them with your passions and purpose. By leveraging your strengths, you can enhance your performance, make meaningful contributions, and create a fulfilling life. Embrace your uniqueness, invest in your growth, and confidently leverage your strengths to unlock your potential.

15 Ways to Earn with Your Talent and Skills

- Start a small business
- Freelancing
- Online Surveys and Market Research
- Renting Out Property
- Content Creation

- Online Tutoring
- Affiliate Marketing
- E-Commerce
- Stock Market and Investments
- Renting Out Possessions
- App Development
- Virtual Assistance
- Photography and Stock Photos
- Online Courses and E-books
- Gig Economy

1. **Start a Small Business:** Identify a product or service you can offer and launch your small business. One can sell handmade crafts

online or provide services like graphic design or copywriting.

2. **Freelancing:** Use your skills and expertise to offer freelance services. You can carry out this service on platforms such as Upwork and Fiverr. They provide an environment for freelancers to connect with clients seeking services such as programming or social media management.

3. **Online Surveys and Market Research:** You can participate in online surveys or market research studies conducted by research groups or organizations. These platforms pay individuals for sharing their opinions and insights.

4. **Rentage of Property:** If you have extra space, consider renting your properties through platforms like Airbnb or VRBO. The

properties can include a spare room, vacation property, or your entire house while you're away.

5. **Content Creation:** If you enjoy creating content, you can start a blog, YouTube channel, or podcast. These platforms through product advertisement, sponsorships, or direct service delivery of content creation, can be rewarding financially.

6. **Online Tutoring:** Share your knowledge and professionalism online through tutorial services. Platforms like VIPKid or Tutor.com link tutors with students seeking help in various subjects.

7. **Affiliate Marketing:** You can earn through affiliate marketing programs. Earn a commission for each sale or referral through your unique affiliate link.

8. **E-commerce:** You may wish to start an online store to sell products. You can create your products or utilize dropshipping to sell products without the need for inventory management.
9. **Stock Market and Investments:** Invest in stocks, bonds, or other investment opportunities. However, you need to carry out your research and understand the financial markets.
10. **Renting Out Possessions:** Rent out possessions or items you own but don't frequently use. You can rent items like cameras, equipment, or even a car. You can use platforms like Turo.
11. **App Development:** Develop and monetize your mobile applications. You can create free

apps with advertisements or charge for premium features.

12. **Virtual Assistance:** Offer virtual assistance services to businesses or individuals. You can be involved in tasks like scheduling, research, email or social media management.

13. **Photography and Stock Photos:** Sell photographs or license them as stock photos. Platforms like Shutterstock or Adobe Stock allow you to showcase and sell your images.

14. **Online Courses and E-books:** Create and earn from online courses or e-books. Platforms such as Udemy and Amazon Kindle Direct Publishing can be used for this purpose. Share your expertise on a specific subject and earn passive income from sales.

15. **Gig Economy:** Take on gigs or short-term projects through platforms like TaskRabbit,

where individuals can hire you for tasks such as moving, assembling furniture, or running errands.

Overcoming Limiting Beliefs and Self-Doubt
Limiting beliefs and self-doubt can prevent individuals from reaching their full potential and achieving their goals. These negative thought patterns can undermine confidence, hinder progress, and create self-imposed barriers. However, with the right strategies and mindset, you can overcome limiting beliefs and self-doubt and unleash your true potential. We will explore tips for overcoming these obstacles and empowering yourself to achieve greatness.

- **Identify and Challenge Limiting Beliefs:** The first step in overcoming limiting beliefs is to become aware of them. Pay attention to your thoughts and identify the beliefs holding you back. Challenge the validity of these beliefs by asking yourself if there is evidence to support them or if they are simply assumptions. Replace negative beliefs with empowering ones that align with your goals and aspirations.

- **Practice Self-Compassion and Positive Self-Talk:** Treat yourself with kindness and understanding, acknowledging that everyone has strengths and weaknesses. Counter negative thoughts with affirmations and inspiring words. Retrospect on your past successes and landmarks, and reinforce a positive self-image.
- **Seek Support from Positive Influencers:** Have supportive and positive influencers

around you. Identify and relate with mentors, coaches, or trusted friends who can provide guidance, encouragement, and genuine feedback. Share your goals and aspirations with them, and allow their belief in you to reinforce your self-belief. Reduce contact with unsupported individuals who may fuel self-doubt.

- **Appreciate Small Wins and Acknowledge Progress:** Celebrate your achievements, no matter how small. Acknowledge the progress you make toward your goals, as it reinforces a sense of competence and builds confidence. Keep a journal or log of your accomplishments, reviewing it regularly to remind yourself of your growth and potential.

- **Focus on Strengths and Positive Attributes:** Shift your focus from weaknesses and limitations to your strengths and positive attributes. Identify and leverage your unique talents and abilities. Acknowledge your areas of strengths and find ways to apply them in pursuit of your goals. Recognize that success often comes from leveraging and expanding upon your existing strengths.

- **Setting Goals and Creating a Plan**

Setting goals and creating a plan to achieve them empowers individuals to turn their dreams into reality. Goals provide direction and motivation to achieve purpose, while a well-defined plan helps transform aspirations into actionable steps. We will look at the importance and strategies of setting goals and the benefits of having a plan to achieve them. By following this road map, individuals can increase their chances of success, maximize their productivity, and ultimately fulfil their aspirations.

- **The Importance of Goal Setting:** Setting goals provides clarity and focus, enabling individuals to identify what they want and create a vision for their future. Goals serve as a road map, guiding actions and decisions and keeping individuals motivated and accountable. They give purpose and meaning to daily efforts and help individuals prioritize their time and resources.

- **The Benefits of Having a Plan:** To have a well-defined plan is crucial for translating goals into reality. A plan outlines specific steps, strategies, and resources to achieve goals. It provides structure and organization, helping individuals stay on track and progress systematically. A plan allows individuals to anticipate challenges, develop contingencies, and allocate resources effectively. It enhances productivity and efficiency by breaking down goals into manageable tasks.
- **Setting SMART Goals:** Setting SMART goals ensures that goals are specific, measurable, attainable, relevant, and time-limit. The goals must be clear without any ambiguity and should have quantifiable criteria to monitor progress

and achievements. Time-limit goals have a stipulated time frame for completion. It discourages laziness and procrastination and factor in accountability.

- **Creating a Detailed Action Plan:** To create a detailed action plan is crucial for turning goals into actionable steps. Simplify the goals into smaller tasks or milestones. Determine the resources, skills, and support needed for each task. Assign deadlines to each step and prioritize them based on necessity. Consider potential obstacles and develop strategies to overcome them. Regularly review and revise the action plan to stay flexible and adaptable.
- **Tracking Progress and Making Adjustments:** Tracking progress is

essential for staying motivated and ensuring goal attainment. Regularly evaluate and measure progress against the set milestones or targets. Celebrate achievements and learn from setbacks. Reflect on the effectiveness of the plan and make adjustments if necessary. Remain open to feedback and continuously assess the alignment of actions with goals.

- **Maintaining Motivation and Accountability:** Maintaining motivation and accountability is vital throughout the goal-setting and planning phases. Stay connected to the purpose and significance of the goals. Find ways to stay inspired, such as visualizing success, creating a vision board, or seeking support from mentors or accountability partners. Hold yourself accountable by regularly reviewing progress, adhering to deadlines, and seeking feedback.

- **Overcoming Challenges and Adapting to Change**: Challenges and unexpected changes are inevitable when pursuing goals. Cultivate resilience and adaptability to overcome obstacles and navigate through change. Be prepared to revise plans, seek alternative strategies, and remain flexible. Embrace setbacks as learning opportunities and use them to refine goals and actions.

Setting goals and creating a plan to achieve them is a transformative process that empowers individuals to realize their full potential. By setting SMART goals, creating a detailed action plan, tracking progress, maintaining motivation, and adapting to challenges can produce concrete achievements. This roadmap to success provides clarity, structure, and direction, allowing individuals to remain focused, productive, and accountable. Embrace the power of goal setting and planning. With a clear vision and well-executed plan, success is inevitable.

Chapter 3

Mastering the Art of Productivity

Productivity is a highly sought-after skill in the world. You may be an entrepreneur, a student, or a professional, and the ability to maximize your output in the limited time available can make a significant difference in achieving your goals. Mastering the art of productivity is not about working longer hours but working smarter and efficiently. You will learn various tips that can help you become a master of productivity, enabling you to unlock your full potential and accomplish more in less time.

- **Set Clear Goals and Priorities:** Goal setting can enhance productivity. Without a clear goal with direction, it is easy to get lost in a sea of tasks and lose sight of what truly matters. Define your long-term goals and then break them into smaller, actionable steps. Create a to-do list or use productivity tools to organize and prioritize your tasks. Focus on the most critical tasks first, and ensure that your energy and effort are towards activities that match your objectives.
- **Display Time Management Skill:** Time management is crucial to mastering productivity. Techniques like Pomodoro

can help you make the most of your time. It guarantees concentration and prevents burnout. You can also apply time blocking to assign and fix time for different activities to ensure you dedicate uninterrupted periods to specific tasks. Additionally, eliminating or minimizing distractions, such as turning off notifications or finding a quiet workspace, can significantly enhance productivity.

- **Harness the Power of Automation and Technology:** Advancements in technology have provided us with numerous tools and Apps that can streamline and automate tasks, saving us time and effort. Identify repetitive tasks in your workflow and explore automation tools that can handle them efficiently. For example, email filters and canned responses can help manage your inbox more effectively. Project management tools like Trello or Asana can aid in organizing and collaborating on projects. Additionally, productivity Apps can assist in time tracking, goal setting, and habit formation. Embrace technology as your ally and leverage it to optimize your productivity.

- **Cultivate Effective Habits and Routines:** Productivity is about implementing strategies and cultivating effective habits and routines. Start by identifying habits that hinder your productivity, such as procrastination or multitasking, and work towards replacing them with more productive alternatives. Create a daily routine and dedicate time to your various activities. Establishing a consistent routine helps condition your mind and body for optimal performance. Regular goal reviews, journaling, and continuous learning can further enhance productivity and personal growth.

- **Optimize Your Environment:** Your environment can play a significant role in determining productivity levels. Take a critical look at your workspace and make necessary adjustments to optimize it. Make sure your workspace is clean, organized, and without distractions. Personalize it with items that inspire and motivate you. Consider incorporating natural light, plants, and ergonomic furniture to create a conducive environment for focused work. Furthermore, establish boundaries and communicate your availability to minimize interruptions from colleagues or family members. Create an environment that supports your productivity and enjoy success.

Mastering the art of productivity is a continuous process that needs self-awareness, discipline, and commitment. Setting clear goals with effective time management, leveraging technology, cultivating productive habits, and optimizing your environment can achieve remarkable results. Productivity is not just about doing more; it is doing the right things. Embrace these strategies and unleash your productivity to create a life of purpose and accomplishment.

The Importance of Productivity in Achieving Success

Productivity is a critical factor that enables an individual to succeed in any endeavour. Productivity can help drive progress, achieve milestones, and ultimately attain success. Let us discuss the significance of productivity and how it contributes to success.

- **Maximizing Output in Limited Time:** Time is a finite resource, and productive individuals understand the value of utilizing it effectively. Productivity enables individuals to maximize their output within the constraints of time. To efficiently manage tasks, set priorities, and avoid time-wasting activities, individuals can accomplish more in less time. This ability to make the most of limited time allows individuals to take on additional responsibilities, pursue multiple goals simultaneously, and capitalize on opportunities that come their way.

- **Enhancing Efficiency and Effectiveness:** Productivity goes beyond busy schedules; it involves working smarter rather than harder. It emphasizes efficient allocation of resources, such as time, energy, and effort, to achieve desired outcomes. Productive individuals focus on tasks that align with their goals and have the most significant impact. They eliminate or delegate non-essential or low-value activities to allow them to channel their energy into activities that yield substantial results. By honing their skills, adopting effective strategies, and leveraging technology, productive individuals continuously seek ways to optimize their performance and achieve outcomes efficiently.

- **Driving Progress and Momentum:** Productivity plays a pivotal role in driving progress and maintaining momentum towards success. When individuals consistently progress towards their goals, it boosts their motivation, confidence, and overall sense of achievement. Productivity provides a sense of purpose and direction and ensures individuals remain focused and committed to their objectives. The ability to split larger goals into smaller, manageable bits and consistently work towards their completion enables individuals to experience a sense of accomplishment and maintain forward momentum.

- **Seizing Opportunities:** Success often involves maximizing opportunities as they arise. Productive individuals identify and maximize opportunities because they have the necessary time, resources, and mental clarity. By staying organized, prioritizing tasks, and having a proactive mindset, they are more attuned to recognizing opportunities that align with their goals. Moreover, being productive allows individuals to respond quickly and effectively to unforeseen circumstances, challenges, or changes in the external environment, enabling them to adapt and capitalize on emerging opportunities.

- **Overcoming Procrastination:** Productivity helps combat procrastination, a common obstacle to success. By adopting effective time-management techniques and developing self-discipline, you can overcome the tendency to delay important tasks and take action when needed.

- **Increased Focus and Concentration:** Being productive requires concentration and focus on tasks. By minimizing distractions and practising techniques like time blocking or the Pomodoro Technique, you can enhance your ability to concentrate and complete tasks more efficiently.

- **Goal Achievement:** Productivity enables you to progress towards your goals and aspirations. By managing your time and resources effectively, you can focus on the tasks that matter most and work towards their completion.
- **Achieving Work-Life Balance:** Productivity is not limited to professional pursuits; it also extends to personal life. Being productive helps individuals achieve a healthy work-life balance, which is crucial for well-being and success. To manage your time and tasks effectively, you should dedicate periods for work, family, relationships, self-care, and leisure activities. A balanced life promotes greater satisfaction, reduces stress, and fosters holistic growth.

Productivity enables individuals to excel in all areas of life, maintaining harmony and fulfilment.

Productivity is the backbone of success, allowing individuals to accomplish more, optimize their efforts, maintain progress, and seize opportunities. To cultivate a productive mindset, adopt efficient strategies, and make the most of available resources, individuals can activate their potential and achieve their goals. Productivity can allow you to make meaningful contributions, reach your goals, and experience fulfilment across all aspects of lives. Embracing productivity as a core principle will pave the way for remarkable achievements and a life of purpose and success.

Tips and Tools for Effective Time Management

Effective time management is a crucial skill that empowers and increases productivity. This section will provide practical tips and tools to help individuals manage time more effectively, allowing them to prioritize tasks, minimize distractions, and optimize productivity.

- **Set Clear Goals and Priorities:** Defining your goals and priorities gives direction and allows you to focus your time and energy on activities that match your goals. Set short-term and long-term goals and split them into actionable bits.
- **Use Time Blocking:** Time blocking is needed to allocate predetermined time

to your activities throughout the day. Start by scheduling blocks of time for essential tasks, meetings, and appointments. Ensure that you set aside time for focused work and breaks to rest. Creating a structured work schedule will enhance productivity and ensure tasks are completed within the designated time.

- **Prioritize and Delegate Tasks:** Not all tasks are of equal importance. Prioritize your tasks based on urgency and significance. Commit yourself to complete high-priority tasks first before the low-priority tasks. Additionally, kindly learn to delegate relevant tasks to free up time for more pertinent issues and responsibilities.

Effective delegation allows you to leverage the strengths and abilities of others and also concentrate on tasks that require your skills.

- **Harness the Power of Technology:** Numerous digital tools and applications such as Google Calendar or Microsoft Outlook are available to enhance time management skills. Project management tools like Trello and Asana enable you to organize and collaborate on tasks and projects. Time-tracking apps like Toggl or RescueTime can provide insights into how you spend your time. Explore different tools to find those that best suit your needs.

- **Practice the Two-Minute Rule:** The two-minute rule states that if a task requires less than two minutes to complete, do it and not postpone it. By promptly addressing these quick tasks, you prevent them from piling up and save time in the long run.
- **Minimize Distractions:** Distractions can significantly hamper productivity. Identify common distractions and take steps to minimize or eliminate them. Turn off notifications on your phone or computer, close unnecessary tabs or applications, and create a dedicated workspace to reduce distractions. You can use productivity apps that block access to distracting websites or set timers for focused work periods.

- **Explore Time Batching:** This involves aggregating similar assignments and working on them simultaneously in a designated time. You can set aside a particular time each day to attend to phone calls, emails, or meetings. This approach allows you to minimize context switching and maintain focus and momentum, which can lead to efficiency and improved productivity.
- **Learn to Say No:** Saying no is essential for effective time management. Understand your limits and avoid overcommitting yourself. Evaluate requests and opportunities against your priorities and goals. If a task or commitment does not align with your objectives or stretches your capacity

too thin, politely decline or negotiate alternative solutions. Learning to say no empowers you to protect your time and prioritize activities that truly matter.

Effective time management can significantly impact productivity and success. Implementing the highlighted strategies like setting clear goals, using time blocking, harnessing technology, minimizing distractions, exploring time batching, and learning to say no, one can take control of one's time and optimize productivity. Try the different techniques and tools to find the ones that work best, and make a commitment to managing your time effectively for long-term success.

Strategies for Staying Focused and Avoiding Distractions

Staying focused has become increasingly challenging in a world filled with constant distractions. However, maintaining focus is crucial for productivity and achieving goals. In this section, you will explore strategies to help you stay focused, minimize distractions, accomplish tasks efficiently and maximize productivity.

- **Create a Distraction-Free Environment:** Designate a specific workspace free of distractions. Remove or minimize potential distractions such as noise, clutter, and personal devices that are not essential for work. You can use noise-cancelling headphones or a white noise machine to block out external disturbances. By creating a dedicated, distraction-free environment, you set yourself up for better focus and concentration.

- **Prioritize and Set Clear Goals**: This is essential for maintaining focus. List out your tasks and set specific, achievable goals for each. Learn to arrange your tasks based on importance and urgency. To know what needs to be done and why, you can direct your attention and energy toward meaningful work, reducing the likelihood of getting side tracked.
- **Practice Time Blocking:** Implement the practice of time blocking to schedule specific periods for focused work. During these dedicated time slots, avoid

distractions by turning off notifications, shutting unused tabs or applications, and setting boundaries with colleagues or family members. This structured approach ensures that you have designated periods for deep concentration and reduces the temptation to engage in unrelated activities.

- **Utilize Productivity Tools:** Leverage productivity tools and apps to stay organized and minimize distractions. You may use task management apps like Todoist or Asana to keep track of your tasks and deadlines. You can use website blockers like Freedom or Stay-Focused to limit access to distracting websites or social media platforms during designated work periods. Additionally, time-tracking apps like RescueTime can provide insights into your digital habits, helping you identify areas where distractions may be creeping in.

- **Practice Mindfulness and Deep Work:** Cultivate mindfulness to enhance focus and attention. Regularly practice meditation or deep breathing exercises to train your mind to stay present and centred. Deep work, a concept popularized by Cal Newport, involves dedicating uninterrupted, focused periods to tackle complex tasks that require deep concentration. Set aside specific time blocks for deep work, during which you eliminate all distractions.
- **Take Regular Breaks:** Paradoxically, taking regular breaks can help you stay

focused in the long run. Working for extended periods without breaks can lead to mental fatigue and reduced attention span. Incorporate breaks into your schedule to allow you to rest and rejuvenate. Use these breaks to stretch, move around, or engage in activities that help clear your mind.

- **Practice Self-Discipline:** Staying focused requires self-discipline and self-control. Be aware of your tendency to get distracted, and work on overcoming the tendency. Develop strategies to resist the temptation of distractions, such as implementing the "five more minutes" rule, where you commit to working for an additional five minutes before allowing yourself a brief break or distraction.

Practice self-accountability by regularly evaluating your progress and adjusting your behaviours accordingly.

By creating a conducive environment, setting clear goals, practising time blocking, utilizing productivity tools, cultivating mindfulness, taking breaks, and exercising self-discipline, individuals can enhance their ability to concentrate on tasks and achieve greater productivity. Apply these strategies consistently, and over time, you will develop the discipline and focus necessary to accomplish your goals efficiently.

21 Ways to Become a Millionaire

Becoming a millionaire is a significant financial goal that many aspire to achieve. While the journey to wealth requires dedication, discipline, and perseverance, it is possible to acquire wealth. 21 strategies are listed to help you build wealth and become a millionaire. These strategies encompass various aspects of personal finance, investing, entrepreneurship, and mindset.

1. **Set Clear Financial Goals:** Define specific and measurable financial goals. Establish a target net worth, income level, or savings milestone to work towards. Having clear goals provides direction and motivation on your path to becoming a millionaire.

2. **Develop a Savings-Plan:** Create a budget that prioritizes savings. Dedicate part of

your income to savings and consistently contribute to a dedicated savings or investment account. This disciplined approach ensures a consistent flow of funds towards wealth-building.

3. **Live Below Your Means:** Adopt a frugal mindset and prioritize saving over excessive spending. Limit unnecessary expenses, avoid lifestyle inflation, and seek value in purchases.

4. **Maximize Income Potential:** Explore opportunities to increase your income. Enhance your skills, pursue promotions or higher-paying job opportunities, or consider starting a side business. Diversifying income streams can accelerate wealth accumulation.

5. **Invest Early and be Consistent:** Start investing as early as possible and make consistent contributions. Take advantage of compounding returns by investing in stocks, bonds, mutual funds, or other suitable investment vehicles. Stay disciplined during market fluctuations and maintain a long-term perspective.

6. **Build a Diversified Investment Portfolio:** Construct a diversified investment portfolio to mitigate risk. Invest across different asset classes, industries, and geographies. This diversification can help shield your wealth from the impact of market volatility.

7. **Educate Yourself on Personal Finance:** Continuously expand your knowledge of personal finance. Understand budgeting,

investing, debt management, and tax planning. The more aware you are, the better you'll be fortified to make sound financial decisions.

8. **Minimize and Manage Debt:** Avoid unnecessary debt and manage existing debt responsibly. Learn to pay off high-interest debts first. Practice responsible borrowing and maintain a healthy credit score.

9. **Leverage the Power of Compound Interest:** Harness the power of compound interest by reinvesting investment earnings. Allow your investment returns to generate additional returns over time, accelerating wealth accumulation.

10. **Embrace Entrepreneurship:** Consider starting your own business or venture.

Entrepreneurship offers the potential for significant wealth creation but requires dedication, diligence, and a willingness to take risks.

11. **Network and Build Relationships:** Cultivate and build a strong network. Attend organizational events, join professional associations, and interact with like-minded professionals. Building relationships can guarantee mentorship or open up valuable opportunities and partnerships.

12. **Persist and Be Resilient:** Persistence and resilience can help you overcome obstacles to wealth. Embrace failures as learning opportunities, adapt to challenges, and maintain a positive mindset.

13. **Seek knowledge to Learn and Improve:** Prioritize your personal and professional development. Continuously acquire new knowledge, skills, and insights. Stay updated on industry trends and developments to remain competitive.
14. **Take Calculated Risks:** Be willing to take calculated risks as you pursue opportunities. Assess risks, weigh potential rewards, and make informed decisions. Calculated risks can yield significant returns and propel you towards your financial goals.
15. **Prioritize Long-Term Thinking:** Adopt a long-term perspective when making financial decisions. Focus on wealth-building strategies that generate

sustainable results over time rather than seeking quick, short-term gains.

16. **Seek Expert Advice:** Consult with financial advisors or professionals who can guide investment strategies, tax planning, and wealth management. Their expertise can help optimize your financial decisions.

17. **Continuously Monitor and Adjust Strategies:** Regularly review your financial progress and adjust your strategies accordingly. Stay informed about changes in the market, adjust your investment portfolio as needed, and adapt to evolving circumstances.

18. **Practice Tax Efficiency:** Optimize your tax planning to minimize the impact of taxes on your wealth accumulation.

Explore tax-efficient investment accounts, deductions, and credits to maximize your after-tax returns.

19. **Give Back and Practice Philanthropy:** Develop a mindset of generosity and consider giving back to society. Support visions you care about through charitable donations or volunteering. Giving back will create a positive impact and also foster gratitude and fulfilment.

20. **Interact with Persons of Like Mind:** Surround yourself with individuals who inspire and motivate you to succeed. Join mastermind groups, seek mentorship, and engage with a supportive community. Positive influences can fuel your drive towards wealth-building.

21. **Stay Committed to Your Financial Journey:** Building wealth requires time

and effort. Stay committed to your financial journey, remain disciplined in your savings and investment practices, and persevere through challenges.

Becoming a millionaire requires a combination of financial strategies, disciplined saving and investing, continuous learning, and a resilient mindset. Implementing these 21 strategies can set you on a path toward building wealth and achieving your financial goals. However, remember that wealth accumulation is a journey that requires time, patience, and adaptability. Embrace the process, stay focused on your goals, and be willing to make adjustments along the way. Ultimately, the journey to becoming a millionaire is not solely about the money; it is about the growth, learning points, and fulfilment that comes with financial success.

Chapter 4

Cultivating Resilience in Achieving Success

Resilience is a vital quality that plays a significant role in achieving success. It is the ability to bounce back, overcome obstacles, and adapt to challenges. Resilience empowers individuals to persevere, maintain focus, and stay committed to goals. In this section, you will learn the importance of resilience in achieving success and discuss strategies to develop and strengthen this valuable trait.

- **Embrace a Growth Mindset:** Developing a growth mindset is fundamental to cultivating resilience. Acknowledge that challenges and failures are part of learning and growth. View obstacles as stepping stones to success and approach them with a solution-oriented mindset. By reframing setbacks as valuable learning experiences, you build resilience and become more adept at navigating challenges.
- **Develop Emotional Intelligence:** Emotional intelligence is the ability to understand and manage emotions effectively. It is a crucial aspect of

resilience. Cultivate self-awareness by recognizing and acknowledging your emotional state in every situation. Practice emotional regulation by developing strategies to cope with stress, anxiety, and other negative emotions. Additionally, foster empathy and build strong relationships to enhance your support system and receive guidance during challenging times.

- **Build a Supportive Network:** Identify and interact with a supportive network of individuals who believe in your potential and provide encouragement. Also, identify mentors, coaches, or like-minded peers who can give guidance, perspective, and emotional support. A support base can help you stay motivated, gain valuable insights, and receive constructive feedback, fostering resilience in your pursuit of success.

- **Practice Adaptability and Flexibility:** Success often requires adapting to changing circumstances and being flexible in approaches. Cultivate adaptability by embracing change, being open to new ideas, and proactively seeking alternative solutions. Develop the ability to pivot and adjust your strategies when faced with unexpected challenges. By maintaining a flexible mindset and being willing to make necessary adjustments, you can navigate obstacles more effectively and bounce back stronger.

- **Set Realistic Expectations:** Setting realistic expectations is crucial for resilience. Understand that the path to success is rarely linear, and setbacks are part of the journey. Set achievable goals and recognize that progress may involve ups and downs. Avoid comparing yourself to others and focus on your growth and improvement. Setting realistic expectations can help you maintain a positive mindset, celebrate small victories, and stay motivated even during challenging times.
- **Practice Self-Care and Well-Being:** Resilience is germane to self-care and well-being. Prioritize your health and engage in activities that replenish your energy, like exercise, healthy eating, and

sufficient rest. Engage in stress management exercises, meditation or mindfulness to cultivate inner calm and resilience. Taking care of yourself ensures you have the strength and resilience to face challenges head-on.

- **Learn from Setbacks and Failures:** Resilience can be developed by learning from setbacks and failures. Instead of dwelling on disappointments, reflect on the lessons they offer. Identify the challenge and areas for improvement, and adjust your approach accordingly. See setbacks as opportunities for growth and development.

Learning from failures can help you become more resilient and better equipped to overcome future challenges. Cultivating resilience is essential for achieving success in any endeavour. Embracing a growth mindset, developing emotional intelligence, building a supportive network, practising adaptability, setting realistic expectations, prioritizing self-care, and learning from setbacks can strengthen resilience and perseverance.

Strategies for Overcoming Setbacks and Failures

Setbacks and failures are inevitable in the pursuit of success. However, how we respond to these challenges defines our ability to bounce back and move forward. This section will highlight strategies for overcoming setbacks and failures.

- **Embrace a Growth Mindset:** This mindset helps individuals view setbacks or failures as opportunities for growth and learning. With a growth mindset, setbacks and failures become stepping stones to success, allowing you to persevere and seek new solutions.
- **Reframe the Situation:** When faced with setbacks or failures, reframe the situation by focusing on the lessons and opportunities it presents. Ask yourself, "What can I learn from this experience?" or "How can I use this setback as a stepping stone for future success?" Shifting your perspective from a negative to a constructive outlook helps you find meaning and purpose in adversity.

- **Analyse and Learn from the Experience:** Take the time to analyse objectively setbacks or failures. Identify factors that contribute to outcomes and reflect on your actions and decisions. Consider what you could have done differently and what lessons you can draw from the experience. Learning from setbacks enables personal growth and equips you with valuable insights for future endeavours.
- **Seek Support and Guidance:** Reach out to your support network during challenging times. Seek guidance from mentors, coaches, or trusted friends and family members. They can provide valuable perspectives, advice, and emotional support. Surrounding yourself

with a supportive community strengthens your resilience and reminds you that setbacks are a shared experience and not a reflection of your worth or abilities.

- **Take Responsibility and Ownership:** Take responsibility for your actions and the outcome of the setback or failure. Acknowledge any mistakes or shortcomings and avoid blame. Taking ownership helps you regain control over circumstances and can proactively work towards finding solutions and improving your approach.

- **Set Clear and Realistic Goals:** After a setback or failure, reassess and refine your goals. Set clear and realistic objectives that match your vision and values. Break down these goals into manageable bits, creating a roadmap for progress. Setting achievable targets helps restore motivation and provides a sense of direction, allowing you to move forward with renewed focus.

- **Cultivate Resilience:** Build resilience by developing coping mechanisms and strategies to navigate setbacks. Cultivate self-care practices such as exercise and mindfulness, and maintain a work-life balance. Practice positive self-talk and challenge negative thoughts that may arise from setbacks. Resilience is not about avoiding failure but bouncing back and learning from it.
- **Persist and Persevere:** You need persistence in the face of setbacks and failures. Stay committed to your goals and

understand that setbacks are temporary obstacles to success. Persevere through challenges, adapt your approach when necessary, and keep taking consistent actions towards your objectives.

- **Celebrate Small Wins:** Acknowledge small victories and celebrate them. Celebrating small wins boosts confidence, provides motivation, and reinforces a positive mindset.
- **Refocus and Adapt:** When setbacks occur, refocus your energy and adapt your approach. Assess what needs to be changed or adjusted to overcome the obstacle. Be open to new strategies, perspectives, and opportunities. Flexibility and adaptability allow you to

navigate unexpected circumstances and find alternative paths to accomplishment. Setbacks and failures are part of the journey towards success. By embracing a growth mindset, reframing situations, learning from experiences, seeking support, taking responsibility, setting clear goals, cultivating resilience, persisting, celebrating small wins, and adapting, individuals can overcome setbacks and failures. Remember, setbacks are not the end but rather an opportunity for growth and eventual triumph.

Building Mental and Emotional Resilience

Building mental and emotional resilience is essential for navigating life's challenges, maintaining well-being, and achieving success. Resilience enables individuals to adapt and thrive in the face of adversity. In this article, we will explore ten valuable pieces of advice for building mental and emotional resilience, empowering individuals to develop inner strength and effectively navigate the ups and downs of life.

- **Cultivate Self-Awareness:** Develop self-awareness by paying attention to your thoughts, emotions, and reactions. Notice how you respond to stress and adversity. Understanding your triggers and patterns empowers you to make conscious choices and take proactive steps towards building resilience.
- **Practice Mindfulness:** Meditation or deep breathing exercises are good for building resilience. Mindfulness helps you stay present, observe your thoughts

without judgment, and cultivate a sense of calm. When you practise mindfulness, you will better manage stress, increase self-awareness, and build resilience.

- **Build a Supportive Network:** Have a supportive network of family, friends, mentors, or support groups. Seek connections with individuals who uplift and encourage you. Sharing your challenges and seeking support from others can provide valuable perspectives, guidance, and emotional strength during difficult times.
- **Develop Coping Strategies:** Identify healthy coping strategies that work for you. Engage in activities such as exercise and journaling that help you relax and recharge. Find healthy outlets to release

stress and manage emotions effectively to build resilience.

- **Reframe Challenges as Opportunities:** Shift your perspective and view challenges as a tool for learning. Reframe setbacks as valuable experiences that can strengthen your resilience. Embracing a positive outlook can help you approach difficulties with a solution-oriented mindset and see them as stepping stones to personal development.
- **Engage in Self-Compassion:** Be kind and compassionate towards yourself and your loved ones. Embrace self-compassion during challenging times, acknowledging that setbacks and failures are part of the human experience. Show yourself

patience and understanding, allowing for healing and growth.

- **Develop Problem-Solving Skills:** You need a problem-solving skill to build resilience. Break down life issues into manageable parts and brainstorm potential solutions. Seek different perspectives and explore creative alternatives. Developing problem-solving skills enables you to approach obstacles with confidence and adaptability.
- **Practice Emotional Regulation:** Learn to regulate your emotions effectively. Develop techniques to manage stress and negative emotions, such as exercises and activities that bring happiness. Emotional regulation helps maintain balance and resilience during difficult times.

- **Foster Optimism and Gratitude:** Cultivate optimism and gratitude. Focus on the positive aspects of situations, even during challenging times. Practice gratitude by reflecting on things you are thankful for, fostering a sense of appreciation and resilience. Optimism and gratitude nourish a positive mindset that allows one to approach difficulties with resilience and hope.

Building mental and emotional resilience is a lifelong journey. By cultivating self-awareness, practising mindfulness, building a support network, developing coping strategies, reframing challenges, practising self-compassion, fostering a growth mindset, developing problem-solving skills, practising emotional regulation, and nurturing optimism and gratitude, individuals can strengthen resilience and thrive in the face of adversity. Resilience is not about avoiding difficulties but developing inner strength to navigate them with grace and determination.

13 Ways to Start a New Business

Starting a new business can be an exciting and rewarding venture. Here are 13 steps to help you get started:

1. **Identify a Profitable Niche:** Research and locate a niche or market segment that aligns with your interests, skills, and expertise. Find a gap or unmet need within that niche and develop a unique value proposition.

2. **Conduct Market Research:** Gather information about your target market demographics, buying behaviours, competitors, and trends. This research will help you understand your customers' needs and preferences.
3. **Develop a Business Plan:** Create a comprehensive business plan that outlines your mission, vision, target market, products or services, marketing strategies, financial projections, and growth plans. A well-crafted business plan serves as a roadmap for your business's development.
4. **Secure Funding:** Determine the financial requirements of your business and explore funding options. The options may include personal savings, loans from

banks or financial institutions, grants, or seeking investors.

5. **Choose a Legal Structure:** Decide on the legal structure of your business, such as sole proprietorship, partnership, or limited liability company (LLC). Consult a lawyer or accountant to determine the most suitable structure for your situation.

6. **Register Your Business:** Register your business name and obtain all licenses and permits required by local and state authorities. This step ensures that you operate legally and protects your business's identity.

7. **Set Up Your Infrastructure:** Establish the necessary infrastructure for your business, including securing a physical location (if applicable), setting up utilities, acquiring

equipment or technology, and establishing communication channels.

8. **Build Your Team:** Identify the key roles and skills required for your business and start building your team. You may hire staff or freelancers or outsource tasks to specialists.

9. **Develop Your Brand Identity:** Create a brand identity that represents your business values, personality, and unique selling proposition. Develop a compelling logo, tagline, and consistent visual and verbal messaging.

10. **Create a Marketing Strategy:** Develop a comprehensive strategy to promote your business and attract customers. Identify the most effective channels to reach your target audience, such as social media,

content marketing, search engine optimization, or advertising.

11. **Launch Your Product or Service:** Prepare your product or service for launch by ensuring it meets quality standards and aligns with customer expectations. Develop a marketing campaign to generate awareness and excitement around your offering.

12. **Establish Customer Relationships:** Focus on delivering excellent customer service and building relationships. Listen to their feedback, address their concerns, and continuously seek ways to enhance their experience.

13. **Monitor, Adapt, and Grow:** Regularly monitor your business performance, track key metrics, and make data-driven

decisions. Stay adaptable and be willing to make necessary adjustments to your products, services, or business model based on market feedback and emerging trends.

Starting a new business requires hard work, dedication, and resilience. Be prepared to face challenges and stay focused on your long-term goals. With careful planning and execution, your new business has the potential to thrive and succeed.

Chapter 5

Building Strong Relationships

Building relationships is a vital component of achieving success. Success requires collaboration, support, and the ability to connect with others effectively. In this article, we will explore the importance of building relationships in the pursuit of success and provide strategies for cultivating and nurturing these relationships.

- Effective communication is the foundation of building relationships. Develop active listening skills, express your thoughts and ideas clearly, and seek to understand others' perspectives. Be open and receptive to feedback and practice empathy to build rapport and understanding. Effective communication fosters trust and collaboration, essential elements for achieving success.
- Surround yourself with a diverse and supportive network of individuals with shared values. Seek mentors, colleagues, or like-minded peers who can provide guidance, motivation, and accountability. A supportive network offers encouragement and doors to

opportunities and resources that can contribute to your success.

- Cultivate authentic connections by being genuine and sincere in your interactions. Show interest in others' lives and work, and be willing to offer your support and assistance when needed. Building authentic relationships based on trust and mutual respect establishes a solid foundation for collaboration and success.
- Emotional intelligence plays a crucial role in building relationships. Develop self-awareness to understand your own emotions and reactions. Practice empathy to recognize and understand others' emotions. Regulate your emotions effectively to maintain harmonious relationships. Cultivating emotional

intelligence will help navigate conflicts, build understanding, and foster strong connections.

- Success often involves working with others towards a common goal. Foster collaboration and teamwork by promoting a culture of cooperation, inclusiveness, and shared accountability. Encourage open communication, value diverse perspectives, and recognize the strengths and contributions of each team member. Building collaborative relationships enhances productivity and achieves collective success.
- Expressing appreciation and gratitude strengthens relationships and creates a positive atmosphere. Acknowledge the efforts and contributions of others,

celebrate their achievements, and express gratitude for their support. Showing appreciation fosters goodwill, motivates others, and builds a sense of camaraderie, ultimately contributing to collective success.

- Trust is the cornerstone of relationships. Be reliable and consistent in your actions and commitments. Follow through on your promises and demonstrate integrity and accountability. Building trust takes time and effort, but it is essential for establishing long-lasting and mutually beneficial relationships that contribute to both individual and shared success.

- Be willing to support and collaborate with others on their journeys to success. Offer your skills, expertise, and resources to help others achieve their goals. By fostering a spirit of collaboration and support, you will contribute to others' success, strengthen your network and enhance your opportunities for growth and achievement.

- Engage in active networking by attending industry events, joining professional organizations, and participating in online communities. Be proactive in building connections and nurturing relationships with individuals who can contribute to your success. Seek opportunities to network, exchange knowledge, and build mutually beneficial partnerships.

- Building relationships requires time, effort, and genuine investment. Prioritize relationship-building activities in your schedule, such as regular check-ins, meetings, or networking events. To nurture relationships, you must stay connected, offer support, and maintain a genuine interest in others' growth and success.

- Building relationships is a valuable asset on the journey to success. By developing communication skills, building a supportive network, cultivating authentic connections, practising emotional intelligence, fostering collaboration, showing appreciation, building trust, offering support, practising active networking, and investing in relationship building, individuals can forge meaningful connections that contribute to their personal and professional achievements.

Maintaining Strong Relationships in Achieving Success

Building and maintaining strong relationships is a critical factor in achieving success. Success is not solely dependent on individual skills or efforts; it often requires collaboration, support, and opportunities that arise through meaningful connections. In this article, we will explore the importance of building and maintaining relationships in the pursuit of success and how they contribute to personal and professional achievements.

- **Collaboration and Synergy:** Strong relationships foster collaboration and synergy. When individuals with diverse skills, experiences, and perspectives come together, they can leverage each other's strengths, pool resources, and generate innovative ideas. Collaboration entails the sharing of knowledge, expertise, insights, and resources.

- **Access to Opportunities:** Building relationships opens doors to opportunities. By cultivating a network of connections, individuals gain access to information, resources, and potential partnerships that can propel their success. Opportunities often arise through referrals, introductions, and recommendations from trusted relationships, providing individuals with a competitive advantage.

- **Emotional Support and Motivation:** Strong relationships provide emotional support and motivation. The journey to success is often challenging and filled with obstacles. To have a support system of individuals who believe in you, encourage you, and provide emotional support during difficult times can make a significant difference. They can offer guidance, lend a listening ear and provide the motivation to persevere through setbacks and maintain focus on long-term goals.
- **Mentorship and Guidance:** Mentorship and guidance from established relationships can accelerate personal and professional growth. Mentors offer valuable insights, wisdom, and advice

based on their experiences. They can guide navigating challenges, making critical decisions, and expanding one's skills and knowledge. A mentor's support and guidance can significantly impact an individual's trajectory towards success.

- **Building a Supportive Ecosystem:** Strong relationships help to build a supportive ecosystem. Surrounding oneself with like-minded individuals who share similar aspirations and values creates an environment that fosters growth and success. Within this ecosystem, individuals can collaborate, inspire, and learn from one another.
- **Access to Diverse Perspectives:** Strong relationships offer exposure to diverse perspectives. Engaging with individuals

from different backgrounds, industries, and cultures broadens one's horizons and challenges conventional thinking. These diverse perspectives provide fresh insights, alternative solutions, and creative approaches to problem-solving. They expand one's knowledge base and enhance adaptability, fostering success in an ever-evolving world.

- **Opportunities for Learning and Development:** Maintaining established relationships provides ongoing opportunities for learning and development. Engaging in meaningful conversations, attending industry events, and participating in professional networks offer platforms for continuous learning and personal growth. Through these relationships, individuals can stay updated with industry trends, gain new skills, and stay ahead of the curve, ultimately contributing to their success.

- **Collaboration and Resource Sharing:** Strong relationships facilitate collaboration and resource sharing. Individuals can leverage their relationships to access shared resources, such as knowledge, expertise, contacts, and financial support. Collaborative endeavours and resource sharing amplify efforts and enable individuals to achieve more than they could singly, leading to increased success.

- **Enhanced Credibility and Reputation:** Building and maintaining relationships enhanced credibility and reputation. Trusted relationships act as social proof, endorsing an individual's capabilities and character. When others perceive you as reliable, trustworthy, and skilled, it opens doors to new opportunities, partnerships, and collaborations. A strong reputation increases visibility and attracts positive attention, ultimately propelling success.

- **Long-Term Sustainability and Well-being:** Strong relationships contribute to long-term sustainability and well-being. Success is not solely about achieving short-term goals but also maintaining them in the long run. Strong relationships provide a support system, a sense of belonging, and opportunities for personal fulfilment. Strong relationships contribute to overall well-being, happiness, and resilience.

Building and maintaining strong relationships is crucial for achieving success. Through collaboration, access to opportunities, emotional support, mentorship, a supportive ecosystem, diverse perspectives, learning opportunities, resource sharing, enhanced credibility, and long-term sustainability provide the foundation for personal and professional achievements. By investing in relationships and nurturing them over time, individuals can create a network of support that propels them towards their goals and enriches their journey towards success.

Strategies for Networking and Building Professional Relationships

Networking and building professional relationships are essential for career growth, personal development, and accessing opportunities. Here are some effective strategies to help you network and build strong professional relationships:

- **Define Your Goals and Purpose:** Clarify your networking goals and the purpose behind building professional relationships. Outline what you hope to achieve through networking, whether finding job opportunities, gaining industry knowledge, or expanding your professional circle. Having a clear vision will guide your networking efforts.
- **Attend Industry Events and Conferences**: Actively participate in industry events, conferences, seminars, and workshops related to your field. These gatherings provide excellent opportunities to meet like-minded professionals, gain industry insights, and establish connections with

individuals with shared interests and goals.

- **Engage in Online Networking:** Leverage online platforms such as LinkedIn, professional forums, and industry-specific online communities. Engage in discussions, share valuable content, and connect with professionals in your field. Online networking allows you to expand your reach, connect with individuals globally, and tap into virtual networking events and webinars.

- **Seek Out Professional Associations:** Join professional associations and organizations related to your industry. These associations often host networking events, conferences, and workshops tailored to specific fields. They offer opportunities to meet professionals, access industry resources, and build relationships with individuals in your field.

- **Offer Value and Support:** Approach networking with a mindset of giving and supporting others. Seek ways to add value to the people you connect with. Share your knowledge, offer assistance, and provide support when possible.
- **Follow Up and Stay Connected:** Following meetings or networking events, follow up with individuals you've connected with. Send personalized messages expressing your interest in maintaining the connection. Stay connected by engaging with their content, sharing relevant resources, and

periodically checking in. Consistent communication helps strengthen relationships over time.

- **Cultivate Authenticity and Rapport:** Build authentic relationships by being genuine and authentic in your interactions. Show a sincere interest in others, actively listen, and ask thoughtful questions. Find common ground and shared interests to build rapport. Authenticity fosters trust and lays the foundation for meaningful professional relationships.

- **Seek Out Mentorship:** Look for mentors who can provide guidance, support, and advice in your professional journey. Seek individuals who have achieved success in your field and share similar values.

Establishing a mentor-mentee relationship can provide valuable insights, help navigate challenges, and open doors to new opportunities.

- **Leverage Existing Connections:** Utilize your existing network to expand your connections. Ask for introductions to individuals who can offer valuable insights or collaborate on projects. By leveraging your current relationships, you tap into their networks and increase your chances of meeting professionals who align with your goals.
- **Maintain a Positive and Professional Image:** Present yourself positively and professionally in all networking interactions. Be mindful of your communication, both online and offline.

Maintain an online presence that reflects your expertise and professionalism. Demonstrating integrity and a positive attitude builds trust and enhances your reputation.

Networking and building professional relationships require intentional effort and a genuine approach. By defining your goals, attending industry events, engaging in online networking, seeking out professional associations, offering value, following up, cultivating authenticity, seeking mentorship, leveraging existing connections, and maintaining a professional image, you can effectively build a professional network that contributes to your career success and personal growth. Remember, building relationships is an ongoing process that requires nurturing and genuine investment.

Cultivating Meaningful Personal Relationships

Building personal relationships is crucial to our lives, bringing joy, support, and fulfilment. Cultivating meaningful personal relationships requires time, effort, and a genuine investment in building connections. Here are some valuable tips to help you foster and nurture meaningful personal relationships:

- **Be Present and Engaged:** When spending time with loved ones, be fully present and engaged. Put away distractions and give them your undivided attention. Listen actively without interrupting or judging. Active listening and genuine interest in their lives show that you value and care about them, deepening the connection.

- **Show Empathy and Understanding:** Seek to understand others' perspectives and emotions. Practice empathy by putting yourself in others' shoes and seeking to understand their perspectives. Validate their feelings and experiences without judgment. Offering support and compassion strengthens bonds and fosters trust.

- **Communicate Openly and Honestly:** Establish open and honest communication with your loved ones. Express your thoughts, feelings, and needs clearly and listen to other people's opinions. Effective communication builds trust and allows for deeper understanding.

- **Practice Forgiveness and Letting Go:** Conflicts and misunderstandings usually arise in any relationship. Practice forgiveness and let go of grudges to maintain healthy and meaningful connections. Holding onto resentment hinders the growth of relationships.

- **Spend Quality Time Together:** Make an effort to spend quality time with your loved ones. Plan activities or outings that allow for shared experiences and create cherished memories. Quality time strengthens bonds and nurtures a sense of belonging.

- **Support Each Other's Growth:** Encourage and support the personal growth and aspirations of your loved ones. Celebrate their achievements, offer guidance when needed, and provide a safe space for them to explore their passions and dreams.

- **Practice Active Appreciation:** Regularly express gratitude and appreciation for the presence and contributions of your loved ones to you. Show them that you value and cherish their presence. Small gestures of appreciation can go a long way in cultivating meaningful connections.

- **Be Reliable and Trustworthy:** Build trust by being reliable and trustworthy. Follow through on commitments, keep confidence, and be dependable. Trust forms the foundation of sustained relationships and fosters a sense of security and intimacy.

- **Nurture Common Interests and Shared Experiences:** Engage in activities and hobbies you and your loved ones enjoy. Shared interests create bonds and provide opportunities for meaningful connections. Participate in activities that foster mutual enjoyment and lasting memories.
- **Celebrate Differences:** Embrace and celebrate the differences in others. Learn from diverse perspectives and foster an inclusive environment.
- **Practice Mindful Communication:** Be mindful of your words and tone. Choose your language carefully and be respectful in your communication.
- **Share Responsibilities:** Distribute responsibilities and tasks fairly within

relationships. Collaborate and work together as a team.

- **Stay Committed:** Building meaningful relationships takes time and effort. Stay committed and invest in nurturing and growing these connections.
- **Practice Self-Care and Boundaries:** Take care of yourself and set healthy boundaries in relationships. Prioritize self-care, as it enables you to show up fully for others.

Cultivating meaningful personal relationships requires genuine effort, open communication, empathy, and shared experiences. Availability, empathy, communicating honestly, supporting growth, spending quality time, practising appreciation, building trust, nurturing common interests, and maintaining boundaries help you create and nurture meaningful connections that bring joy and fulfilment to your life and the lives of your loved ones.

Chapter 6

Creating a Positive Mindset

A positive mindset is a powerful tool that can significantly impact our journey toward success. It shapes our thoughts, emotions, and actions, influencing how we perceive challenges, setbacks, and opportunities. Cultivating a positive mindset involves adopting optimistic beliefs, embracing resilience, and maintaining a constructive outlook. We will explore the importance of having a positive mind and provide practical strategies to develop and sustain it.

Our thoughts shape our reality. With the power of thoughts, we can cultivate a positive mindset. Pay attention to your self-talk and challenge negative or limiting beliefs. Replace them with positive, empowering affirmations. Choose thoughts that align with your goals, strengths, and potential. Over time, this conscious effort will rewire your mind to focus on the positive aspects of any situation.

A positive mindset is a mental attitude or perspective on optimism, gratitude, and constructive thinking. It involves consciously choosing positive thoughts, beliefs, and emotions, even in challenging situations. A positive mindset allows individuals to approach life with resilience, enthusiasm, and a belief in their abilities to overcome obstacles and achieve their goals.

At its core, a positive mindset involves cultivating a positive and empowering self-image. It begins with self-awareness and self-reflection, understanding one's thoughts, emotions, and beliefs. A positive mind recognizes negative patterns and consciously replaces them with positive and empowering thoughts. This process requires effort and practice to reframe negative experiences and interpretations into more positive and constructive ones.

A positive mindset embraces the power of optimism. Optimism is the belief that favourable outcomes are possible and setbacks are temporary and manageable. It is not about denying reality or ignoring challenges but finding solutions, learning from failures, and focusing on possibilities and opportunities. Optimistic individuals view setbacks as learning experiences and stepping stones towards success. They maintain a hopeful outlook, seek positive alternatives, and take proactive steps towards their goals.

Gratitude is another crucial aspect of a positive mindset. It involves recognizing and appreciating the blessings, opportunities, and positive aspects of one's life. Gratitude shifts the focus from what is lacking to what is present, fostering contentment and joy. Practicing gratitude can enhance well-being, resilience, and overall satisfaction with life. It reminds individuals to acknowledge the small victories, express appreciation for others, and cultivate a sense of abundance.

A positive mindset also involves embracing constructive thinking. It entails reframing challenges as learning points for growth and finding solutions rather than dwelling on problems. Constructive thinking helps promote a problem-solving approach and encourages individuals to seek alternative perspectives, think creatively, and focus on what they can control. It emphasizes learning from mistakes, adapting to change, and maintaining a forward-thinking mindset.

Moreover, a positive mindset is in tandem with self-belief and self-confidence. It involves developing a strong belief in one's abilities, strengths, and potential. Individuals with a positive mindset trust themselves to handle challenges and setbacks, knowing they possess the inner resources and resilience to overcome obstacles. They cultivate self-confidence through self-affirmation, visualization, and celebrating their achievements, no matter how small.

The benefits of a positive mindset extend beyond personal well-being. It can positively impact relationships, career success, and overall quality of life. Positive-minded individuals tend to attract positive experiences and build supportive connections with others. They radiate optimism and inspire those around them. In the workplace, a positive mindset contributes to productivity, creativity, and effective collaboration. It fosters a culture of resilience, motivation, and continuous improvement.

Impact of a Positive Mindset on Achieving Success

- **Optimistic Outlook:** A positive mindset fosters an optimistic outlook. It allows us to see challenges as avenues for growth and learning. Instead of being overwhelmed by obstacles, we approach them with a solution-oriented mindset. This optimism fuels resilience, creativity, and a willingness to take risks.

- **Enhanced Self-Belief:** A positive mindset strengthens our self-belief and confidence. When we believe in our abilities and potential, we are more likely to set ambitious goals, take on challenges, and persevere in adversity. Self-belief fuels motivation and determination, enabling us to overcome obstacles and reach higher levels of achievement.

- **Increased Resilience:** Resilience is the ability to bounce back from setbacks. A positive mindset helps us develop resilience by reframing failures as learning experiences and setbacks as temporary obstacles. Instead of being discouraged by failure, we view it as an opportunity to grow, adapt, and improve. This resilience enables us to persist in challenges and maintain a forward momentum.
- **Improved Problem-Solving Skills:** A positive mindset enhances our problem-solving skills. When faced with challenges, we approach them with a proactive and solution-focused mindset. We seek

creative solutions, explore alternative perspectives, and think outside the box. This mindset opens us up to new possibilities and enables us to overcome obstacles more effectively.

- **Expanded Growth Mindset:** A positive mindset aligns with a growth mindset. It encourages us to believe in the power of continuous growth and improvement. We embrace challenges, seek feedback, and view failures as opportunities for learning and progress. With a growth mindset, we are more open to taking on new challenges, acquiring new skills, and expanding our capabilities.
- **Increased Emotional Well-being:** A positive mindset promotes emotional well-being. Positive thinking and

optimism reduce stress, anxiety, and negative emotions. When we have a positive mind, we approach tasks enthusiastically and maintain a sense of fulfilment. This emotional well-being fosters productivity, creativity, and the ability to stay focused, all of which are critical for success.

- **Enhanced Resilient Response to Failure:** Failure is an inevitable part of the journey toward success. A positive mindset enables us to respond to failure in a resilient manner. Instead of getting discouraged or giving up, we see failure as a stepping stone to success. We learn from our mistakes, adapt our strategies, and keep moving forward. This resilient response to failure enables us to persevere and ultimately achieve our goals.

- **Improved Relationships and Support:** A positive mindset influences our interactions with others and the relationships we cultivate. When we have a positive outlook, we attract like-minded individuals who can support us on our journey. Positive relationships provide encouragement, collaboration, and valuable feedback. They create a supportive network that can propel us toward success by offering guidance, resources, and opportunities.
- **Attraction of Opportunities:** A positive mindset has a magnetic effect on opportunities. When we radiate positivity, we attract opportunities and people who

align with our goals. Employers, clients, and collaborators are attracted to individuals with a positive mindset. Individuals with a positive mind are proactive, solution-oriented, and motivated.

- **Long-lasting Happiness and Fulfillment:** Ultimately, a positive mindset leads to long-lasting happiness and fulfilment. Success is about achieving targeted goals and finding joy and satisfaction in the journey. A positive mind allows us to appreciate the process, celebrate small victories, and find meaning in our endeavours. This sustainable happiness and fulfilment are measures of success.

Strategies for Cultivating Positivity and Optimism

Cultivating positivity and optimism is a powerful practice that can transform our mindset and enhance our well-being. Here are some strategies to help you cultivate positivity and optimism in your daily life:

- **Practice Gratitude:** Start each day by expressing gratitude for the things you have in your life. Reflect on the positive aspects and blessings, no matter how small they may seem. Keep a gratitude journal and regularly write down three things you are grateful for. This practice shifts your focus to the positive and trains your mind to notice and appreciate the good things around you.

- **Challenge Negative Thoughts:** Become aware of negative thoughts and self-talk patterns. Whenever you think negatively, challenge those thoughts by asking yourself if they are rational or helpful. Replace negative thoughts with positive, empowering affirmations. Over time, this practice rewires your brain to focus on the positive and diminishes the power of negative thinking.
- **Surround Yourself with Positive Influences:** Spend time with positive, supportive, and uplifting people. Surround yourself with individuals who inspire and motivate you. Engage in activities, read books, or listen to podcasts that promote positivity and personal growth. By immersing yourself in a

positive environment, you fuel optimism and create a supportive network that reinforces your positive mindset.

- **Practice Mindfulness and Meditation:** Engage in mindfulness and meditation practices to cultivate present-moment awareness and foster a positive mindset. Set aside time each day to sit in silence, focus on your breath, and observe your thoughts and emotions without judgment. This practice enhances self-awareness, reduces stress, and allows you to respond to challenges with clarity and positivity.

- **Find the Silver Lining:** Train your mind to find the silver lining in challenging situations. Instead of dwelling on the negatives, look for the lessons, growth opportunities, or hidden blessings.

Shifting your perspective helps you reframe challenges as stepping stones to success and cultivates a positive outlook even in difficult circumstances.

- **Practice Self-Compassion:** Be kind and compassionate toward yourself. Treat yourself with the same understanding and support you would offer a dear friend. Whenever you have setbacks or failures, practice self-compassion and acknowledge that everyone makes mistakes as a growth and learning process. Self-compassion helps you bounce back with resilience and maintain a positive attitude.
- **Set Realistic Goals:** Set realistic and achievable goals that align with your values and aspirations. Break them down

into smaller, manageable steps. This approach allows you to experience a sense of progress and accomplishment, which fuels positivity and optimism. Celebrate each milestone along the way, no matter how small, and use them as reminders of your growth and potential.

- **Surround Yourself with Positive Visuals:** Create a positive environment by surrounding yourself with uplifting visuals. Display inspiring quotes, images, or affirmations in your workspace or home. Fill your surroundings with things that evoke positive emotions and remind you of your goals and aspirations.

- **Practice Acts of Kindness:** Engage in acts of kindness toward others. Random acts of kindness, offering help, appreciation, or compliments, will positively impact others and uplift your spirit. Acts of kindness foster positive emotions, strengthen relationships, and contribute to a sense of interconnectedness and positivity.

- **Practice Self-Care:** Prioritize self-care to nurture your physical, mental, and emotional well-being. Take care of your physical health through regular exercise, proper nutrition, and adequate sleep. Engage in activities that bring you joy and relaxation. Taking care of yourself can replenish your energy and maintain an optimistic mindset.

Dealing with Negative Thoughts and Emotions

Life is a beautiful tapestry of experiences, but it is not immune to challenges that test our resilience. Negative thoughts and emotions are an inevitable part of the human condition, often arising from various sources such as setbacks, conflicts, or self-doubt. How we handle these thoughts and emotions contributes to our well-being and happiness. In this note, we will explore practical advice on navigating the storm of negative thoughts and emotions, empowering you to cultivate a positive mindset and find inner peace.

- **Acknowledge and Accept:** The first step in dealing with negative thoughts and emotions is acknowledgement. It is natural to experience negativity, and it does not define your entire being. Allow yourself to feel those emotions without judgment or resistance. By accepting their presence, you can initiate the process of healing and transformation.

- **Practice Mindfulness:** Cultivating mindfulness is a powerful tool to observe and manage negative thoughts and emotions. Mindfulness involves being fully present in the moment and paying attention to your thoughts and feelings without attachment. Through mindfulness, you can create a space between yourself and your negative thoughts, allowing for greater clarity and self-awareness. Practice meditation, deep breathing, or journaling to foster mindfulness in your daily life.

- **Practice Self-Awareness:** Develop the habit of being aware of your thoughts and emotions. Notice when negative thoughts arise and how they make you feel. By being aware, you can start to detach yourself from them and prevent them from overwhelming you.
- **Challenge Negative Thoughts:** Negative thoughts often stem from distorted beliefs or cognitive biases. Challenge these thoughts by examining their validity and replacing them with more rational and positive alternatives. Consider the evidence supporting or contradicting your negative thoughts. Adopting a balanced perspective can help you reframe situations and prevent spiralling into negativity.

- **Surround Yourself with Positive Influences:** The people we surround ourselves with impact our thoughts and emotions. Seek out individuals who radiate positivity, empathy, and understanding. Engage in meaningful conversations, share your concerns, and gain insights from their perspectives. Additionally, surround yourself with uplifting and inspiring content, such as books, podcasts, or motivational videos, to serve as sources of encouragement.
- **Self-Care and Well-being:** Taking care of yourself physically, mentally, and emotionally is essential for managing negative thoughts and emotions. Prioritize self-care activities that promote relaxation, such as exercise, adequate

sleep, a balanced diet, and engaging in hobbies you enjoy. Set realistic goals, celebrate your achievements and practice self-compassion. Remember that self-care is not selfish but a foundation for personal growth and well-being.

- **Seek Support:** Do not hesitate to seek support from loved ones or professional help when needed. Opening up about your struggles with trusted individuals can provide a fresh perspective and emotional support. Therapists or counsellors can offer valuable guidance and strategies to cope with negative thoughts and emotions. Remember, reaching out for help is a sign of strength, not weakness.

- **Journaling:** Write down your negative thoughts and emotions in a journal. Documentation will help you know the patterns and triggers of your emotions. Use the journal to highlight positive experiences, accomplishments, and things you are grateful for to balance out negativity.
- **Engage in Positive Practices:** Cultivate habits and practices that promote positivity and emotional well-being. Engage in activities like gratitude, journaling, and random acts of kindness that bring you joy. Set aside time for relaxation, reflection, and self-reflection.
- **Embrace Imperfections:** Recognize that imperfections are part of the human experience. Embrace your flaws and learn

from your mistakes. Instead of dwelling on perceived shortcomings, focus on personal growth and self-improvement. Treat setbacks as opportunities for learning and development. Embracing imperfections enables you to approach life with resilience and self-acceptance.

Remember that dealing with negative thoughts and emotions is an ongoing process. Be patient and kind to yourself as you cultivate a more positive and resilient mindset. With practice and perseverance, you can develop effective strategies to navigate negative thoughts and emotions and lead a more balanced and fulfilling life.

Chapter 7

Embracing Continuous Learning

Embracing continuous learning in achieving success is a mindset and approach that goes beyond simply acquiring knowledge or skills. It involves cultivating a lifelong commitment to personal and professional development, adapting to change, and consistently seeking new opportunities to grow and improve.

It also means adopting a growth mindset, believing in the potential for growth and improvement in all areas of life. This mindset encourages a willingness to step outside comfort zones and embrace challenges as learning points. Success in today's rapidly evolving world requires adaptability, openness to change, staying curious, and embracing new ideas and perspectives. It involves recognizing that the skills and knowledge that brought success in the past may not be sufficient for the future. By actively seeking new information and learning experiences, individuals can adapt to changing circumstances and stay ahead in their fields.

Continuous learning involves self-reflection and a willingness to critically assess one's strengths, weaknesses, and areas for improvement. It requires an honest evaluation of skills, knowledge gaps, and growth. Through self-reflection, individuals can identify inadequacies and develop strategies to overcome challenges.

Learning does not end with formal education or reaching a certain level of expertise. It involves a commitment to ongoing personal and professional development throughout one's life. Learning can be through various means, such as attending workshops, conferences, and seminars, pursuing certifications, reading books, engaging in online courses, or seeking mentorship opportunities.

Continuous learning fosters a mindset of curiosity and a drive to find creative solutions to problems. It encourages individuals to seek new knowledge and perspectives to approach challenges. By continuously learning and expanding their skill set, individuals can contribute innovative ideas and approaches to their work and personal lives, leading to increased success and fulfilment.

Embracing continuous learning involves recognizing the value of networking and collaborating with others. By connecting with a diverse range of individuals, sharing knowledge, and engaging in meaningful conversations, individuals can gain new insights, expand their perspectives, and foster opportunities for growth and success. Collaborative learning environments provide fertile ground for creativity, learning from others' experiences, and building valuable relationships.

In summary, embracing continuous learning in achieving success means adopting a growth mindset, staying adaptable, engaging in self-reflection, committing to lifelong learning, fostering problem-solving and innovation, and embracing collaboration. By embodying these principles, individuals can be relevant, continuously improve their skills and knowledge, and unlock their full potential for personal and professional success.

Continuous Learning in Achieving Success

The pursuit of success requires more than innate talent and initial education. Continuous learning, the ongoing process of acquiring new knowledge, skills, and perspectives, is pivotal to succeeding. It empowers individuals to adapt to changing circumstances, overcome challenges, and unlock their full potential. This essay explores the significance of continuous learning in achieving success, emphasizing its role in personal and professional growth, adaptability, innovation, and self-fulfilment.

Personal and Professional Growth:

Continuous learning fuels personal and professional growth by expanding horizons and deepening knowledge. It enables individuals to acquire new skills, refine existing ones, and broaden their understanding of the world. Through learning, individuals can challenge themselves, overcome limitations, and unlock their full potential. Continuous learning enhances critical thinking, problem-solving, and decision-making, providing a competitive edge in various domains. Furthermore, continuous learning promotes self-confidence and a sense of accomplishment. As individuals acquire new knowledge and skills, they gain the confidence to tackle new challenges, take on greater responsibilities, and pursue higher aspirations.

Adaptability and Resilience:

In an era of rapid change, adaptability is crucial for success. Continuous learning nurtures adaptability by fostering a growth mindset and a willingness to embrace new ideas, technologies, and ways of thinking. It allows individuals to stay ahead of the curve and remain relevant in their respective fields. By continually acquiring new knowledge and skills, individuals can adapt to emerging trends, overcome obstacles, and seize opportunities. Moreover, continuous learning enhances resilience. It equips individuals with diverse tools and perspectives, enabling them to navigate uncertainty and bounce back from setbacks.

Innovation and Creativity:

Continuous learning is a catalyst for innovation and creativity. Exposure to new ideas, perspectives, and domains of knowledge sparks creativity and encourages out-of-the-box thinking. Learning from diverse fields fosters cross-pollination of ideas, leading to breakthrough innovations.

Continuous learning also encourages a culture of experimentation and risk-taking. As individuals gain new knowledge, they are more likely to explore uncharted territories and challenge conventional wisdom. This willingness to take calculated risks and explore innovative solutions paves the way for success and distinguishes individuals in their respective fields.

Self-Fulfillment and Well-Being:

Continuous learning contributes to self-fulfilment and overall well-being. Engaging in learning activities that align with personal interests and passions brings joy, purpose, and fulfilment. It nurtures a lifelong love for learning and intellectual curiosity, ensuring that success is not solely measured by external achievements but also by personal growth and satisfaction. Additionally, continuous learning enhances overall well-being. It promotes mental agility, boosts self-esteem, and reduces the risk of cognitive decline. Learning also provides opportunities for social connection and collaboration, fostering a sense of belonging and fulfilment.

Continuous learning is the driving force behind personal and professional success in an ever-changing world. It facilitates personal and professional growth, enabling individuals to develop new skills, refine existing ones, and unlock their full potential. Continuous learning nurtures adaptability, ensuring individuals can thrive amidst uncertainty and embrace new opportunities. Moreover, continuous learning cultivates innovation and creativity, leading to breakthrough ideas and solutions. It instils self-fulfilment, fostering a lifelong love for learning and personal growth. By embracing continuous learning, individuals embark on a transformative journey toward success with achievements, personal growth, adaptability, innovation, and well-being.

Continuous learning is an essential compass, guiding individuals towards success, fulfilment, and a meaningful life. By embracing continuous learning, individuals are well-equipped with the tools, knowledge, and adaptability necessary to navigate the complexities of the modern world and forge their path to success.

Strategies for Developing a Learning Mindset

Developing a learning mindset and acquiring new knowledge and skills are essential for personal and professional growth. Here are some strategies to cultivate a learning mindset and effectively acquire new knowledge and skills:

- **Embrace Curiosity:** Cultivate a sense of curiosity and a hunger for knowledge. Approach learning with an open mind, constantly asking questions and seeking answers. Curiosity fuels the desire to explore new subjects and motivates active engagement in the learning process.
- **Set Learning Goals:** Define clear learning goals to provide direction and focus. Determine what knowledge or skills you

want to acquire and set specific, achievable goals. Break down larger goals into smaller, manageable milestones to track progress and maintain motivation.

- **Develop a Learning Plan:** Create a structured learning plan that outlines the steps and resources needed to achieve your learning goals. Identify relevant courses, books, online resources, or workshops that can provide the necessary knowledge and skills. Organize your learning activities to align with your schedule and allow for consistent progress.
- **Diversify Learning Approaches:** Explore different learning approaches to cater to your preferred learning style and maximize retention. Experiment with

various methods such as reading books, taking online courses, attending workshops, participating in hands-on projects, or seeking mentorship. Mix and match these approaches to create a well-rounded learning experience.

- **Practice Active Learning:** Engage actively in the learning process. Take notes, summarize key concepts, and ask questions. Participate in discussions, seek opportunities for application and practice, and reflect on your learning experiences. Active learning enhances comprehension, retention, and the ability to apply knowledge effectively.

- **Seek Diverse Perspectives:** Expand your knowledge and understanding by seeking diverse perspectives. Engage in conversations with people from different backgrounds and areas of expertise. Join study groups, online communities, or forums related to your areas of interest. Actively listen and respect differing viewpoints, as they can provide valuable insights and challenge your assumptions.

- **Embrace Failure and Learn from Mistakes:** Embrace failures and setbacks as opportunities for growth. Learn from mistakes, analyze what went wrong, and identify areas for improvement. Adopt a growth mindset that views failure as a stepping stone toward success. Adjust your approach, persevere, and apply the lessons learned from past experiences to future endeavours.

- **Practice Consistency and Discipline:** Learning is a lifelong journey that requires consistency and discipline. Set aside dedicated time for learning and make it a regular part of your routine. Even short daily learning sessions can accumulate substantial knowledge over time. Prioritize learning and treat it as a non-negotiable commitment.

- **Reflect on Your Learning Journey:** Regularly reflect on your learning journey to assess progress, celebrate achievements, and identify areas for further development. Journaling or maintaining a learning portfolio can help track your growth, document key insights, and reflect on how new knowledge and skills have impacted your personal or professional life.

- **Share and Teach Others:** Share your knowledge and skills to solidify your understanding and contribute to the learning community. Teach what you have learned and mentor aspiring learners.

Staying Up-to-date with Industry Trends and Advancements

By implementing these strategies, you can foster a learning mindset, continuously acquire new knowledge and skills, and embark on fulfilling personal and professional growth. Learning is a lifelong pursuit, and every step taken towards expanding your knowledge and skill brings you closer to achieving your goals and unlocking your full potential. Staying up-to-date with industry trends and advancements is crucial for professional growth, maintaining a competitive edge, and making informed decisions. Here are some practical tips to help you stay current in your industry:

- **Follow Industry Publications and Websites:** Subscribe to relevant industry publications, newsletters, and websites. These sources often provide valuable insights, news updates, and analysis specific to your field. Set aside time regularly to read and stay informed.
- **Engage in Professional Associations and Networks:** Join professional associations and attend industry conferences, seminars, or webinars. These events provide opportunities to network with peers, share knowledge, and learn about the latest trends from experts in the field.

- **Leverage on Social Media:** Follow influential figures, thought leaders, and companies in your industry on social media platforms like LinkedIn, Twitter, and Facebook. These platforms often share industry news, research findings, and thought-provoking articles.
- **Participate in Online Forums and Communities:** Engage in online forums, discussion boards, and industry-specific communities. These platforms allow you to connect with professionals in your field, ask questions, share insights, and stay updated on the latest industry discussions.
- **Continuous Learning:** Invest in professional development by pursuing relevant courses, certifications, or workshops. Online learning platforms

like Coursera, Udemy, or LinkedIn Learning offer a range of courses to enhance your skills and knowledge.

- **Set Up Google Alerts:** Create Google Alerts for industry-specific keywords, topics, or key players. This way, you'll receive email notifications whenever new information or news is published online.
- **Engage in Thought Leadership:** Establish yourself as a thought leader by sharing your expertise through blogging, writing articles, or giving presentations. By staying engaged in industry discussions, you'll deepen your understanding and develop a reputation as someone knowledgeable in your field.
- **Join Online Communities:** Participate in online forums, LinkedIn groups, or Slack

channels focused on your industry. These communities provide a platform for professionals to exchange ideas, share resources, and discuss emerging trends.

- **Network and Attend Industry Events:** Attend industry conferences, trade shows, and networking events. These gatherings offer opportunities to connect with industry leaders, gain insights from keynote speakers, and build valuable relationships.

- **Follow Key Influencers and Thought Leaders:** Identify influential figures and thought leaders in your industry and follow them on social media, subscribe to their blogs, or listen to their podcasts. These individuals often share valuable insights and forward-thinking ideas.

- **Read Research Papers and Case Studies:** Stay informed about the latest research papers and case studies relevant to your industry. Academic journals, research institutions, and industry-specific publications often publish these valuable resources.
- **Join Webinars and Online Events:** Take advantage of webinars and virtual events that provide industry-specific insights and discussions. Many organizations and companies host online events that are easily accessible and convenient to attend.
- **Monitor Competitors:** Keep an eye on your competitors' activities, product launches, and innovations. Monitor their websites, social media presence, and press releases to understand the direction of the

industry and identify areas where you can differentiate yourself.

Chapter 8

Enjoying a Life of Success

Embracing a life of success involves adopting a mindset and certain behaviours and habits that support personal and professional growth. Here are some key aspects to consider:

- **Clarity of Purpose:** Clearly define what success means to you. Identify your passions, values, and long-term goals. A clear sense of purpose will guide your decisions and actions towards achieving success.

- **Goal Setting:** The goal must be SMART (specific, measurable, achievable, relevant, and time-bound). The goals should align with the purpose. Break the goals into smaller bits to make them manageable and track progress. Regularly review and adjust the goals as needed.

- **Positive Mindset:** Cultivate an optimistic mindset. Believe in your abilities and strengths. Embrace challenges as learning points for growth and learning. Replace negative self-talk with positive affirmations. Surround yourself with positive influences and inspirational role models.

- **Continuous Learning:** Commit to lifelong learning and personal development. Stay curious and open-minded. Read books, attend seminars or workshops, take online courses, and engage mentors or coaches to guide you. Develop new skills and knowledge that align with your goals.
- **Self-Discipline:** Practice self-discipline to stay focused and committed to your goals. Set priorities, manage your time effectively, and avoid distractions. Establish healthy habits and routines that support your success. Learn to overcome procrastination and stay motivated.
- **Resilience and Perseverance:** Success often requires resilience and the ability to bounce back from setbacks. Embrace failures as learning opportunities and

view obstacles as temporary challenges. Develop coping strategies to deal with stress and adversity. Stay persistent and never give up on your dreams.

- **Networking and Collaboration:** Build a network of like minds to support and inspire you. Surround yourself with mentors and motivated people who can offer guidance, support, and opportunities. Collaborate with others to leverage their expertise and resources.

- **Financial Management:** Take charge of your finances and develop good financial habits. Create a budget, save and invest wisely, and manage debt responsibly. Set financial goals aligned with your overall vision of success. Seek knowledge in personal finance and make informed decisions.

- **Work-Life Balance:** Strive for a healthy work-life balance. Prioritize self-care, including physical exercise, proper nutrition, and sufficient rest. Make time for family, friends, hobbies, and activities that bring you joy and fulfilment. Avoid burnout by setting boundaries and creating time for relaxation and rejuvenation.

- **Gratitude and Mindfulness:** Cultivate gratitude and practice mindfulness in your daily life. Appreciate and celebrate your achievements. Take time to reflect on your progress and express gratitude for the opportunities and support you receive.

Being mindful helps you stay present and fully engaged in each moment.

Embracing a life of success is a continuous journey that requires commitment, self-reflection, and constant growth. Remember that success is personal and can be defined in various ways. Stay true to your values and aspirations as you navigate your path to success.

Success Codes for Daily Living

Embracing a life of success is within your reach. By incorporating the following success codes into your daily life, you can create a foundation for personal and professional growth:

- **Code of Purpose:** Discover your purpose and align your actions with it. Take time to reflect on your passions, values, and long-term goals. Let your purpose guide your decisions and infuse meaning into everything you do.
- **Code of Belief:** Believe in yourself and your abilities. Develop unwavering confidence that you have what it takes to succeed. Banish self-doubt and negative thoughts, replacing them with empowering beliefs that fuel your progress.

- **Code of Action:** Success requires consistent action. Break down your goals into actionable steps and commit to them. Embrace a bias towards action, and be committed to the small steps, that can lead to significant achievements.
- **Code of Growth:** Embrace a growth mindset and see challenges as learning points for learning and development. Continuously expand your knowledge, skills, and perspectives. Seek feedback, learn from failures, and constantly evolve to unlock your full potential.
- **Code of Resilience:** Cultivate resilience to overcome obstacles and setbacks. View failures as stepping stones on the path to success. Build your emotional strength,

bounce back from adversity, and persist in the face of challenges.

- **Code of Discipline:** Practice self-discipline and establish habits that support your goals. Create routines, prioritize tasks, and eliminate distractions. Stay committed to your goals, even when it requires sacrifice and perseverance.
- **Code of Relationships:** Surround yourself with positive and supportive individuals who inspire and challenge you. Cultivate meaningful relationships, seek mentors, and collaborate with like-minded achievers. Build a network that uplifts and empowers you on your journey.
- **Code of Learning:** Commit to lifelong learning and personal growth. Embrace

curiosity, seek knowledge, and stay open to new ideas. Continuously expand your horizons and acquire skills that propel you forward.

- **Code of Balance:** Strive for balance in all areas of your life. Prioritize self-care, maintain healthy relationships, and find harmony between work and personal life. Nurture your physical, mental, and emotional well-being to sustain long-term success.

- **Code of Gratitude:** Cultivate gratitude for the present moment and the progress made. Celebrate achievements, big and small. Express gratitude for the opportunities, resources, and support that come your way. Cultivating gratitude brings joy and attracts more abundance into your life.

By embracing these success codes and integrating them into your daily life, you can create a foundation for success. Remember, success is a journey, not a destination. Embrace the process, stay committed, and strive for growth and fulfilment. Your future of success awaits, so step into it with confidence and determination.

Key Concepts Covered in this Book

Mindset: This success book helps to cultivate a positive and growth-oriented mindset. It encourages readers to develop a belief in their abilities, embrace challenges as learning points for growth, and maintain a positive attitude even in the face of adversity.

Goal Setting: Setting clear and specific goals is a concept in success literature. The book may guide how to set meaningful goals, break them down into actionable steps, and create a plan for achieving them. It may also emphasize the importance of regularly reviewing and adjusting goals as necessary.

Persistence and Resilience: Persistence and resilience are required to succeed. The book may highlight the significance of staying committed to one's goals and persevering through obstacles and setbacks. It may offer strategies for building resilience, such as developing coping mechanisms, seeking support, and learning from failures.

Self-Discipline: Success literature frequently emphasizes the role of self-discipline in achieving goals. The book may discuss techniques for developing self-discipline, such as creating daily routines, prioritizing tasks, and overcoming procrastination. It may also stress the importance of staying focused and avoiding distractions.

Continuous Learning and Improvement:

Successful individuals are often avid learners. The book may emphasize how to acquire new knowledge and skills, stay updated on industry trends, and seek personal and professional growth opportunities. It may encourage readers to invest in self-education, seek mentors, and embrace lifelong learning.

- **Time Management:** Effectively managing time resonates in the success literature. The book may provide strategies for prioritizing tasks, eliminating time-wasting activities, and maximizing productivity. It may also highlight the importance of balancing work and personal life, setting boundaries, and practising self-care.

- **Networking and Relationships:** Building a network and cultivating positive relationships can contribute to success. The book guides on networking strategies, effective communication, and relationship-building skills. It may emphasize the importance of collaboration, seeking mentors, and surrounding oneself with supportive individuals.

- **Financial Management:** Many success books address the importance of financial literacy and management. Some advice on budgeting, saving, investing, and creating multiple income streams. The book may stress the significance of financial independence and planning for the future.

- **Taking Action:** A key message in success literature is the importance of taking action rather than just acquiring knowledge. The book may encourage readers to step out of their comfort zones, overcome fear and procrastination, and consistently take small steps towards their goals. The book may address the value of perseverance and learning in success and failure.
- **Gratitude and Mindfulness:** Some success books focus on the power of gratitude and mindfulness in achieving happiness and fulfilment.

They may encourage readers to appreciate what they have, practice mindfulness and self-reflection, and develop a positive and grateful mindset.

Note: The concepts mentioned here are general and may vary across success books. The concepts covered in a particular success book may depend on the author's focus and approach.

Additional Resources for Readers

Here are some additional resources that can support readers in their journey towards success:

1. **Books**:

- "**The 7 Habits of Highly Effective People**" by Stephen R. Covey

- "**Mindset: The New Psychology of Success**" by Carol S. Dweck

- "**Atomic Habits**" by James Clear

- "**Think and Grow Rich**" by Napoleon Hill

- "**The Power of Now**" by Eckhart Tolle

- "**Grit: The Power of Passion and Perseverance**" by Angela Duckworth

- "**The Miracle Morning**" by Hal Elrod

- "**The Compound Effect**" by Darren Hardy

- "**Start with Why**" by Simon Sinek

- "**The 5 AM Club**" by Robin Sharma

2. **Podcasts**:

- "The Tony Robbins Podcast"

- "The Tim Ferriss Show"

- "The School of Greatness" by Lewis Howes

- "The Mindvalley Podcast"

- "Happier with Gretchen Rubin"

- "The GaryVee Audio Experience" with Gary Vaynerchuk

- "The James Altucher Show"

- "The Robin Sharma Mastery Sessions"

- "The Brendon Show" with Brendon Burchard

3. **Online Courses and Platforms**:

- Coursera: Offers a range of online courses on personal development, leadership, and specific skills.

- Udemy: Provides a list of courses on various topics, including success, productivity, and self-improvement.

- **LinkedIn Learning:** Offers a collection of courses taught by industry professionals on business, personal development, and leadership skills.

- **Mindvalley:** Provides online courses and personal growth programs taught by experts in various fields.

- **TED Talks:** Features inspiring talks on various subjects, including success, motivation, and personal growth.

4. **Websites and Blogs**:

- Success.com: Offers articles, videos, and resources on personal development, entrepreneurship, and leadership.

- Lifehack.org: Provides practical tips and advice on productivity, personal growth, and success.

- **Brain Pickings:** A blog that explores ideas from various disciplines, including psychology, philosophy, and literature, to inspire personal growth and creativity.

- Forbes.com: Publishes articles on success, leadership, entrepreneurship, and career development.

These resources can provide valuable insights, tools, and inspiration to continue the journey towards success. Remember to choose resources that resonate with your goals and interests, and apply the knowledge gained to your life.